Eugène Ionesco

By the same author

PLAYS VOLUME 1
The Lesson, The Chairs, The Bald Prima Donna, Jacques
PLAYS VOLUME 2
Amedee, The New Tenant, Victims of Duty
PLAYS VOLUME 3
The Killer, Improvisation, Maid to Marry
PLAYS VOLUME 4
Rhinoceros, The Leader, The Future is in Eggs
PLAYS VOLUME 5
Exit the King, The Motor Show, Foursome
PLAYS VOLUME 6
A Stroll in the Air, Frenzy for Two
PLAYS VOLUME 7
Hunger and Thirst, The Picture, Anger, Salutations
PLAYS VOLUME 8
Here Comes the Chopper, The Oversight, The Foot of the Wall
PLAYS VOLUME 9
Macbett, The Mire, Learning to Walk
PLAYS VOLUME 10
Oh What a Bloody Circus, The Hard-Boiled Egg, Ionesco and his Early English Critics
PLAYS VOLUME 11
The Man With the Luggage, The Duel, Double Act, Why do I Write?
THREE PLAYS
The Killer, The Chairs, Maid to Marry
NOTES AND COUNTERNOTES
(Essays on the Theatre)
PRESENT PAST PAST PRESENT
(Thoughts and Memoirs of Eugene Ionesco)
WHY DO I WRITE?
(An Essay in *Gambit 32*)
THE HERMIT
(A Novel)

In preparation

ANTIDOTES
(Articles, Polemics and Pamphlets)

PLAYS
VOLUME XII

Eugène Ionesco

JOURNEYS AMONG THE DEAD
(Themes and Variations)

Translated from the French by Barbara Wright

JOHN CALDER : LONDON
RIVERRUN PRESS : NEW YORK

Voyages chez les morts was originally published by
Editions Gallimard, Paris, 1981

This translation first published in 1985 by
John Calder (Publishers) Limited 18 Brewer Street, London W1R 4AS
and simultaneously by
Riverrun Press Inc. 175 Fifth Avenue, New York, NY 10010

BRITISH LIBRARY CATALOGUING IN PUBLICATION DATA
Ionesco, Eugene
Plays.
Vol. 12
I. Title II. Ionesco, Eugene. Journeys among the dead.
842'.914 PQ2617.06
ISBN 0-7145-3956-2

LIBRARY OF CONGRESS CATALOGUING IN PUBLICATION DATA
Ionesco, Eugene.
Journeys among the dead.

Translation of: Voyages chez les morts.
I. Title.
PQ2617.06V6813 1985 842'.914 83-22986
ISBN 0-7145-3956-2

Typeset in Times Roman 9/10 pt by Gilbert Composing Services,
Leighton Buzzard and Printed and bound in Great Britain at
The Camelot Press Ltd, Southampton

Journeys Among the Dead *(Voyages chez les morts)* was first performed in Paris at the T.N.P. in December 1982. It was directed by Roger Planchon, and the cast were:

Jean Carmet
Colette Dompietrini
Thérèse Quentin
Francoise Lugagne
Claude Lochy
Gérard Darrieu
Patricia Karim
Jean Leuvrais
Marc de Jonge
André Reybaz
Michèle Moretti
Rebecca Potok
Janine Berdin
Frida Caussin
Chantal Crochet
Fabrice Manzagol
Claude Meunier
Alain Neddam
Francoise Perret
Chantal Reynaud
Charles Sadoyan
Frédérique Turcato
Maurice Waldmann

CHARACTERS

JEAN
JEAN'S GRANDFATHER: LEON
ERNEST: JEAN'S UNCLE
GRANDMOTHER, THE OLD WOMAN
JEAN'S FATHER
JEAN'S MOTHER
THE FATHER'S SECOND WIFE:
  MADAME SIMPSON, HELENE
    HER TWO BROTHERS:
      PAUL, THE CAPTAIN
      PETER, THE TOP CIVIL
      SERVANT
JEAN'S SISTER: LYDIA
JEAN'S WIFE: ARLETTE
(JEAN confuses them)
LOUIS (JEAN'S FALSE FRIEND)
ALEXANDRE (JEAN'S FRIEND)
  HIS WIFE, VIOLETTE
GEORGES (JEAN'S CHILDHOOD
FRIEND)
Also THE FILM-MAKER, VILLAGERS,
WOMEN, ETC.

THE GYPSY GIRL

Set. The stage is divided by a partition, in which there is a door. Another possibility would be for the stage not to be divided into two, but simply to have a door, or a door-frame, in the middle. On the right-hand side, lying on a makeshift bed, an OLD MAN *wearing a skull cap. On the other side, a slightly* YOUNGER MAN, *sitting on another makeshift bed, reading the paper. On both sides, a chair and a table. Enter* JEAN, *left. Without stopping in the first room, he opens the door and goes into the second one, where the* OLD MAN *is lying.*

JEAN: Hallo, Grandfather.
THE GRANDFATHER. I am your maternal grandfather, but I want you to call me by my christian name: Léon.
JEAN. Hallo, Léon.
THE GRANDFATHER. Why are you looking at me like that? I was seventy-four when I died, and I died thirty years ago, if you remember. You were very young.
JEAN. You look furious. And yet you were very nice to me when you were alive. You used to take me to the cinema. The first time I went up the Eiffel Tower, it was with you. Isn't Grandmother with you?

THE GRANDFATHER *remains silent.*

JEAN. Isn't Emma with you?
THE GRANDFATHER. She died a widow; she's free.
JEAN. You don't often see her, then! Now I look at you, I didn't realize I was so like you; the same eyebrows, the same colour eyes, the same rather big nose.
THE GRANDFATHER. Leave me alone. I'm thinking about my invention.
JEAN. Still your inventions. They never came to anything when you were alive. Do you really think that now . . .
THE GRANDFATHER. Go and see Ernest, my son, your uncle, in his room.
JEAN. I'll be back.
THE GRANDFATHER. They've taken everything away from me. They won't even allow me to smoke my pipe.

He t[illegible]s over and faces the wall. JEAN *pretends to knock on the door.*

JEAN. May I?
ERNEST. Come in.

JEAN *goes in.*

JEAN. So you live with Grandfather, now?
ERNEST: Who gave you my address?
JEAN. Hallo, Ernest.

ERNEST. Call me Uncle. I asked you how you got my address?
JEAN. What's the matter with you both? Was it dying that made you so furious?
ERNEST. I'm not dead. I've reached the age of ninety, I could almost be my father's father. I quite simply decided to call it a day and settle for being ninety. I don't want to be any older.
JEAN. Have you got a brush? The only way I could get here to Grandfather and you was along some very muddy lanes. And it was raining a little. I'm a bit drenched, but the worst of it is that my shoes and the bottom of my trousers are dirty, and then, as all the houses are white and low, I had trouble in recognizing yours. Yours and Leon's, seeing that you live with him.
ERNEST. You haven't answered my question. Who gave you my address?
JEAN. I don't remember. I don't remember. My mother, maybe.
ERNEST. She couldn't have known it. She went before I did. I never see her. I've no news of her. The family don't like me. And when I think of all I did for them! I found jobs for the whole family. I helped them, but whenever things began to look up and they were on the road to fame and fortune, that was the last I saw of them. Well then—who gave you my address? I don't want anyone to know it. I've always considered other people, but the only person I want to consider now is myself.
JEAN. And you don't know, either, where Aunt Suzanne is? She may know my mother's address. Because it's my mother I'm looking for. It's such a long time since I saw her. I don't want her to think I've forgotten her. I'd like to take her some presents, some flowers.

Ah yes, who gave me your address? Maybe I found it of my own accord? Maybe those muddy tracks, those low houses, inspired me. I told myself that that was the sort of place she liked to live in. She was always moving house, and she always looked for ground floors or basements.

She was the one I was looking for, but you're the one I've found. These low houses with low ceilings, white, but rather dirty, they really are what the family likes.
ERNEST. My brother André was the only person who knew my address. I told him not to give it to anyone, not to anyone, anyone at all. I haven't heard anything of him since.
JEAN. He's an octogenarian, since you want to know how old he is now, but he's in good health.
ERNEST. Yes, and as you see, I'm badly dressed, I'm dirty, my black frock coat is completely threadbare, it's shiny with wear. I didn't want you to see me in this state. After all I've done for the human race.

Injustice! Injustice reigns. I have just about enough money to afford to buy the paper once a week. So I don't really know what's going on. I look like a tramp, but I still have my pride and my independence.
JEAN. You couldn't change, Uncle.
ERNEST. No one can buy me.
JEAN. I've brought some money; a lot. I can give you some, seeing that you're her brother.

JEAN *pulls a wad of notes out of his pocket.*

Here—this is for you and Grandfather. There must be at least six hundred ten-thousand-franc notes, ten thousand new francs.

ERNEST *(who doesn't look grateful).* That'll do for the time being. But it's not enough, you must bring me some more.

JEAN. I remember now how I found your address, or at least which direction it was in. I'd been following you along the streets in the town, I'd lost track of you. But before that, I'd seen you going from house to house, from shop to shop. It was odd. On business, no doubt. I didn't want you to see me so I hid round a corner, but then you'd disappeared, you'd escaped me. How did I manage to find you again? Someone, but who?—someone had come part of the way with me, and he told me which way to go.

ERNEST *(having counted all the notes)*: There really are six hundred.

JEAN *(exiting, left)*: I'll be back, but I must try and find her.

ERNEST *goes into* THE GRANDFATHER'S *room, the banknotes in his hand.*

ERNEST. Look, Léon, I've got some money, Victor has given me this, he's paid me back some of what he owes me.

THE GRANDFATHER. I don't think his name is Victor.

ERNEST. What does it matter.

THE GRANDFATHER *gets up, sits on the edge of the bed and looks at the money.*

THE GRANDFATHER. These banknotes are rubbish. They aren't legal tender in our village. Or anywhere else, for that matter.

Set. No 3D set. A chair, a table.

Characters. THE FATHER. ANOTHER MAN *of about fifty. The* OTHER MAN *is sitting at the table, on which there is a briefcase.* JEAN *enters from the right.*

THE FATHER. Have you come to visit me? I wasn't expecting you. Is it really me you've come to see? No, it's her, isn't it?

JEAN. The thing that surprises me most, in my travels, is when I discover towns, towns I'd never even heard of. It's true I was never very good at geography, but I did learn a little at school. And then all of a sudden there's a new town in the middle of the desert! It must be a French colony. It's very harmonious. It has squares which aren't too big, streets which aren't too narrow, boulevards which aren't too wide, well-proportioned houses, neither too high nor too low; their apartments are obviously comfortable, they have balconies. There weren't many people in the streets, probably because the inhabitants would rather stay indoors, where they have everything they need.

THE FATHER. I must have heard about that country. Yes, of course I have; my brother, who was a great geographer and who died very young, drew a map of it. It is indeed a former French colony, it's in the north of China. The men are great riders, people call them 'The Last Horsemen of the Occident'. And yet they live in the Far East. Extremes meet. You didn't see them because they must have been out in the fields when you were there.

JEAN. I came across that country by pure accident at the end of my journey, at one of the ends of my journey. You say it's in the north of China?

THE FATHER. It's called Bogandi, its capital is called Bocal, it's in the Bocala plain, in the middle of the steppes.

JEAN. How come, then, that it was by the sea, the ocean? I went round a corner and suddenly saw the sea; it was as blue as the Mediterranean, and there was even a port.

THE FATHER. It *wasn't* me you came to find. But what do I care—I'm beyond bitterness.

JEAN. The sea at the end of the street was like . . . the street sloped a bit, like they do in San Francisco, apparently, and all of a sudden I saw the sea, with boats . . . Ah, look—it was like that.

A big blue river appears in a very bright light on the back wall, with plants, and very green trees.

Look—it was like that.

The pictures disappear.

THE FATHER. I knew you'd come, and I knew it wouldn't be for me. But I tell you, I really don't care. The new authorities banned all barristers from the bar, apart from three or four, of whom I was one. I've always been a sensible man; I obeyed them. I defended the accused they told me to defend, but I kept within the limits they prescribed.

JEAN. Who could you have defended? You weren't allowed to defend anyone. On the contrary: you accused your clients.

THE FATHER. You're wrong, all of you are wrong. You've been brainwashed by the other side's propaganda. I defended the postmen who came out on strike because of the heat. I supported their claims. But it would have been abnormal for me not to defend the State criminals. Later, the barristers' profession was abolished. But as I had obeyed the authorities they were good to me, they recycled me.

JEAN. They recycled you into the police?

THE FATHER. No, they recycled me into the novel, the realist novel. We are a branch of the Ministry for the Police, we're subsidised by the Ministry for the Police, but we aren't policemen. I'm not a policeman. The proof of that is that I get censored. They cut a few overlong passages in my novels here and there—very little, really. I write stream-of-consciousness novels, but their stream isn't as blue as the Danube, or as the ocean you saw, or thought you saw, in Boganda.

He takes an enormous packet out of the drawer in the table.

Look, this is the first chapter, it's a grey novel.

JEAN. Bumf, red tape, you're a bureaucrat.

THE FATHER. It isn't my politics you hold against me, it's the fact that I divorced her.

JEAN. You abandoned her.

THE FATHER. I'm sorry I can't give you her address. She's disappeared, I took her to the station. She wouldn't tell me where she was going. All I know is that she'd reserved a couchette.

JEAN. If it was a wagon-lit train, its destination must have been shown somewhere. You could have asked someone at the station. I think you were glad to see her go, you did everything you could to get her to leave, you didn't try to stop her. You only had to say one word.

THE FATHER. She's never written to me.

JEAN. She was being tactful.

THE FATHER. Did she ever write to *you*?

JEAN. I didn't get her letters, but she did write to me, I know she did, I have proof. Yes yes; mental proof.

THE FATHER. She must have gone a long way away. She got to a place where you can't see anyone any more, neither with your eyes nor by any kind of technology.

She abandoned *us*.

JEAN. No, it was you. You wanted to remarry.

THE FATHER. I am alone. My second wife is dead. Everyone thought she was still alive and had been a widow for a long time. You see how wrong people can be.

An old-fashioned four-poster bed appears on the stage, with a canopy and closed curtains. Two men, whom we shall call PETER *and* PAUL, MADAME SIMPSON's *two brothers, push the bed to the middle of the stage.*

(THE FATHER). You'll see.

PETER *and* PAUL *pull the curtains back and the bed appears, with a dead woman in it. There are lighted candles at all four corners of the bed.*

There you are: there's the proof.

JEAN. Is this a joke?

THE FATHER. Certainly not. This corpse is the living proof of that. Those are her brothers: Peter and Paul.

PETER (*to* JEAN). Do you recognize me? You were very young.

PAUL. We heard you'd become a celebrity. We were proud of you when we heard you'd won the Davis Cup.

PETER *(pointing to the dead woman in the bed).* As you see, my sister is dead.

PAUL. Yes, my sister is dead.

PETER. Hélène, our older sister, the beauty of the family.

THE FATHER. Everyone has a right to remarry, to separate, to remarry. There was no point in holding it against her. She didn't get anything out of the inheritance–and neither did I. I paid all the money to the State. Luckily, my books sell well. They're even paid for in advance. Sometimes I write them, and Peter or Paul signs them. At other times I sign them, and Peter or Paul writes them.

PETER. A trifraternal co-operative society.

PAUL. We always managed to keep in with all the successive governments.

JEAN (*to* THE FATHER). I don't believe you. You do it all, you write it all, as you always did. And the others take advantage of it. A family of robbers, of gangsters.

THE FATHER. How dare you speak to me like that?

JEAN. What about you, how dare you lie? How did you dare deceive her and rob her, the way you robbed me?

THE FATHER. I didn't owe you anything. Everything I got was through my own efforts, no one ever helped me.

JEAN. *I* don't need your help, but she did, she needed it, and it was your duty to help her.

PETER. You aren't going to come to blows!

PAUL. It isn't nice, it isn't right, to make such a spectacle of yourselves in the presence of a dead woman.

PETER. She's out of it now.

THE FATHER. How beautiful she is, in spite of her age and her white hair. Look at her, she isn't as pale as she was when she was alive.

PETER (*to* JEAN). You were bad at physics and chemistry, you had to have coaching.

THE FATHER. I paid.

JEAN (*to* PETER *and* PAUL). I can't forgive him, because I don't know whether she forgave him.

PETER. The most precious possession, is life.

PAUL. That's what they used to tell us in cadet school.

JEAN. I shall still, still go on looking for her, and when I find her I shall ask her what she still thinks about it. That's if she does still think about it. She might well have forgotten all about it.

Set. A very low door in the middle of the back wall. At first the stage is dark. When the lights come up, three beds or divans become visible, and also TWO WOMEN, *whose voices have been heard at the beginning of this scene.*

Sound of steps, and bumps, of someone outside.

FIRST WOMAN. You'll have to bend down a bit, sir, to get in.
Ah yes, the door isn't very high. Bend down.
Mind your head. Put the light on, sir, if you can't see. The switch is just

over the door hole. Try and find it, sir, grope for it, you'll get it in the end. Try hard. It'll give us some light, too. You've got it, I think.

The lights come up. The TWO WOMEN *are wearing identical masks. At the back of the stage, flat on his stomach,* JEAN *is crawling in through the tiny door, preceded by his hat, which rolls over on the stage for a few instants.*

Come in, sir, come in.
SECOND WOMAN. Come on in.

JEAN *is in. Still flat on his stomach, he drags himself over to his hat and picks it up. He stands up.*

FIRST WOMAN. You haven't hurt yourself?
JEAN. Why do you stay in the dark?
SECOND WOMAN. Because the light can only be switched on or off from the outside. Like you did. People pass by our door on horseback. When they see that the door is too small to come through on horseback, they turn the light off, to annoy us.
FIRST WOMAN. But others, who have kind hearts, switch it on again.
SECOND WOMAN. We're dependent on both sorts, according to whether they're charitable or cruel.
JEAN. Why do you put up with living in this windowless room? . . . I've been looking for her for quite a long time.
FIRST WOMAN. Is it your mother you're looking for?
JEAN. You both look like her. Could one of you be my mother?
FIRST WOMAN. We all look alike. The ones who belong to the community, that is.
SECOND WOMAN. We aren't even relations, no sir, we aren't her sisters. The only things we have in common are spiritual affinities and resemblances.
FIRST WOMAN. She may come. She's gone shopping.
SECOND WOMAN. She left a fortnight ago.
FIRST WOMAN. Oh no, she was here this morning.
SECOND WOMAN. Only this morning? And it already feels like a fortnight?
FIRST WOMAN. She's sure to be back.
JEAN. May I wait?
SECOND WOMAN. Then she will be back. You may wait.
JEAN. I don't know whether we're talking about the same person.
FIRST WOMAN. We could make you some pancakes.
SECOND WOMAN. We've run out of flour.
JEAN. Don't go to any trouble. Your ceiling is very low, too.
FIRST WOMAN. The rent's reasonable.
JEAN. But she must be somewhere.
FIRST WOMAN. I can't think why she wanted to leave. She stayed here for days, for a week, for months, for years, and then, all of a sudden . . .
JEAN. She didn't tell you she was expecting someone?
SECOND WOMAN. No, but she couldn't have known, the post is very bad these days. And anyway, did you write and tell her you were coming?

JEAN. The post is so bad these days.
FIRST WOMAN. I understand.
SECOND WOMAN. She may have gone away for some time.
JEAN *(uneasy and sad).* Perhaps she went away just because she had a feeling I was coming? I've never done her any harm, except by omission.
FIRST WOMAN. We can't intervene in problems of that sort.
SECOND WOMAN. She may have gone to the other provinces to see her friend Julienne—the one who owns the beautiful black castle. She'd had some happy times at that castle, she wanted to see it again before it was pulled down.
JEAN. The black castle? You mean the white castle?
FIRST WOMAN. And yet she certainly was here, a moment ago. Perhaps she's gone for good.
JEAN. Do you really think she's gone for good?

Set. A rather sordid room. In one corner, an old armchair, in which THE FATHER *is sitting. A chair, and, to the right of the stage, a table with drawers.*

Sitting in his armchair, THE FATHER *keeps looking at his wrist watch.*

THE FATHER. He's late, of course, and I'm not surprised. He was always late. He always got bad marks at school. How did he manage to get through university? Bad at Greek, bad at science! And yet he finally passed all his exams. I wanted him to be an engineer! He would never listen to me. He was always against me. What a generation! Eternal accusations; he never understood me. He despised my friends, and my new family.

Enter JEAN.

JEAN. You again! For years now you've been perpetually in my dreams, you and your wife and my mother and your brother-in-law. But before, for dozens of years before, I'd stopped dreaming about you all. Why do I keep coming back to you? What does it mean? That I'm going to join you? That we haven't finished settling our accounts? Always having to go back to those appalling beginnings!
THE FATHER. It's because you're not interested in the world any more.
JEAN. I still exist! I get worse and worse at contending with the sound and the fury. I pretend to be interested in it, but I'm fed up with the whole business.
THE FATHER. And yet you've got on, as they say. You've lived quite an intense life, a very intense life, even. You've become a celebrity.
JEAN. I'm older than you, now. And yet when I see you, when I'm with you, I'm still the unhappy child you used to bully, and beat. You disparaged me because of my mother, who had never done you any harm

and whom you'd abandoned. Luckily, I was able to get away from you when I was seventeen. What could a father like you have done for me?—you even hit your servants. And yet it's true that you did occasionally show me a sort of vague affection, you were sometimes proud of me when I'd had a social success. When politics turned me into a pariah, the ignoble politics of your country, you too treated me like a pariah. You never stood up against either the approval or the disapproval of society, of your society. But as you see, I got the better of you. Because I had the luck and the courage never to obey you. Though no one can say you didn't make a success of the life you lived behind the scenes. You were well thought of by the Freemasons, the Democrats, the Left, the Right, the Fascist governments, the Iron Guard, and finally by the Communist regime.

THE FATHER. I was reasonable, and I was self-effacing.

JEAN. Not for philosophical reasons. It wasn't for philosophical reasons. It was to feather your own nest. Though it didn't do you any good in the end, either in your private life or with your wife, your second one, who couldn't bear you any longer and who used to make her niece sleep between you and her, so you couldn't touch her. The idiot girl with the big feet. The only time I approved of you was when I heard, after your death, that you'd taken a mistress, your gypsy servant. I remember seeing you at the cinema with her one afternoon, I pretended not to recognize you, but I already had my suspicions.

THE FATHER. Working my fingers to the bone, permanently weighed down by guilt, because I wasn't a brute, whatever you may think. She was the joy of my life. The one and only.

JEAN. You bought her a house; it can't be much use to her now, she must be dead, like you. It's a pity we didn't have more confidence in each other. You could have told me about it. You could have taken me for a drink with her. The only person worth knowing in your entire circle.

THE FATHER. Oh, let bygones be bygones, it's all dead and buried, now. Forget your resentment against all those people and families; they're all dead and buried, now.

JEAN. If you all come back to me in my dreams, it must mean that I don't resent you so very much. The problem hasn't been resolved. Wars and upheavals separated us. We were never able to discuss things. Why do I still come to see you in my dreams? You've been dead a long time. I shall soon join you. But even so, I shall still be the son, even when I'm on the other side. I shall still find it difficult to come and see you, you've barricaded yourself in the tombs of your second wife and your brothers-in-law, those crooks . . . —are they really crooks? They were spiteful, stupid, commonplace—though maybe no more so than everyone else—and when I'm in my tomb I shall be beside my wife and my sister, your daughter . . . Unless my wife and I are much farther away, with my daughter—though she will only join us a good deal later! We shall be in other countries that we'd thought were better. That we'd thought were better.

THE FATHER. The very earth will shake. The whole world will be convulsed. Even souls may finally be killed. Oh, come on, you haven't much longer to exist, either; let me have a look at what you've done, at what you've written.

JEAN. All right, I'll show you.

He stands up, goes over to the table, opens some drawers and pulls out some sheets of paper. THE FATHER *follows him.* THE SON *opens another drawer and takes out a bundle of old papers.*

THE FATHER. That's all it amounts to: a few pages in an exercise book, a few scribbles on odd bits of paper; however hard I look, there's nothing legible. You even tried your hand at drawing. I always told you, though, that you're no good at drawing, and no one can make head or tail of what you call your literature. There are some As, and Bs, and Cs, and Xs—nothing that adds up to anything . . . And bits of paper, and signatures . . . And to think that some people have taken this stuff seriously! There's nothing in it, my child, you haven't left any sort of message, you've simply written bird-brained gibberish, bits of words, semblances of sentences. Perhaps you took yourself for a prophet, a witness, an analyst of the situation. You don't create any recognizable situations: it's all a void.

JEAN. I did imagine, for a while, that I'd contributed something, but there isn't anything. For quite some time now, though, I've realized that it was all nothing but hog-wash, putrid hog-wash.

THE FATHER. Don't worry, no one has ever managed to do anything, the world doesn't belong to anyone. The world belongs to Satan, unless God finally snatches it out of his hands, for God is the only one who can give meaning to the creation that Satan has corrupted, and defiled and destroyed. One day, perhaps, it will all be cleansed and repaired, and make some sense to us.

JEAN. I want to introduce two of my friends to you.

Enter TWO WOMEN.

They appear in my dreams. That's because they want you to get to know them, they want to make you laugh.

The TWO WOMEN *kneel down on the ground facing one another, and play at being chickens. The first goes 'cot cot codac' the second goes 'cocorico'. They continue this sort of game, this sort of ballet, for some time, while* THE FATHER *and* THE SON *are speaking.*

THE FATHER. Your friends are very much alive.

JEAN. Yes, I thought they'd appeal to you.

THE FATHER. What are they? They look like chickens. Yes, they're real chickens, not ghost chickens.

JEAN. No; they're ladies playing at being chickens.

Enter, from the back, a FAT WOMAN.

THE FATHER. You recognize her, don't you? That's my second wife, your stepmother.
THE STEPMOTHER. Get out, chickens, or I'll get my turkeycock to chase you out.

The TWO WOMEN *stop.*

You shouldn't bring chickens into the houses of people who have been dead for so long.

Another WOMAN *arrives, right, with a broom, and pushes the two chicken-women out. They are still playing as they disappear.*

At last we're alone together.
JEAN (*to* THE FAT WOMAN). You ought to look after yourself.
THE FATHER. We don't feel depressed or sad, here, we've left sadness and joy behind.
JEAN. You are ghosts, but you have a memory.
THE FATHER. We shall be dissolved, but not straightaway; only when the others come, and when the towns and the plains have become empty.

Outside, faint cries, faint bursts of machine gun fire can be heard.

THE FATHER. Yes, we can still hear all that, but it doesn't bother us any more; it's muted, we only half-listen.
THE STEPMOTHER. But I still have my word to say, I never said it all the time I was alive, I said other words that weren't my own, I have my word to say, my word to say.

Enter JEAN, *right. At the same time a woman enters, left. The two characters meet in the middle of the stage.*

THE WOMAN *(who must be the mother).* Are you Jean?
JEAN. I think so.

He feels in his pockets and brings out an identity card.

According to this card, I think that's who I am.

He looks around him.

I can't see a mirror.
THE MOTHER. Here's a little pocket mirror.
JEAN *(taking it).* This is a good mirror. I do in fact recognize my features. A little the worse for wear, but they're still my features.
THE MOTHER. You haven't aged, you haven't changed, you ought to recognize yourself more easily.

JEAN *(looking more carefully).* Yes, that's true. I have the same wrinkles, they're congenital, I already had them when I was a very young child.

He gives the mirror back.

Where are we, then, here?—are we in Bucharest? That's where I think it is.
THE MOTHER. Yes. It is Bucharest.
JEAN. I seem to recognize this house.
THE MOTHER. It's the flat that belongs to your father's second wife, your wicked stepmother.
JEAN. But you—who are you? I seem to recognize you, I believe I've known you for a very long time, but who are you exactly? Are you my wife, are you my daughter? Are you my sister? You're one of those three people, I'm sure of that. My father is rich, you know, he gives me an enormous amount of money.
THE MOTHER. You were never capable of earning any yourself, with your poems. Those poems aren't worth much.
JEAN. Fortunately, my father spoils me. Sometimes he's too harsh, at other times he's very generous. I've already spent five hundred thousand francs, I've got a hundred thousand left, I shall ask him for some more if he's still in a good mood. At the moment, he's spoiling me.

JEAN *looks around him.*

Why are there so many empty bedrooms in this house? You can take your choice, and sometimes sleep in one room, sometimes in another. What a lot of things to eat there are in the cupboards!
THE MOTHER. You eat too much, you never stop eating, you'll get fat.

JEAN *looks on the table.*

JEAN. What are all those books piled up there? They're old books, very old books.

He picks one up.

It's in strange writing, they're hieroglyphics.
THE MOTHER. They're religious books, in old Romanian.
JEAN. It's hardly comprehensible; in fact, it's completely incomprehensible.
THE MOTHER. You don't know Romanian any more. You've forgotten Romanian, even modern Romanian.
JEAN. No I haven't, I do recognize a word here and there. There are crosses. I can still read it, I recognize the word 'angel'.
THE MOTHER. Don't eat all the plums.
JEAN. And these cards? They're tarot cards, aren't they?
THE MOTHER. I told you to stop looking in the cupboards and the fridge. You've had enough to eat; that'll do.

JEAN *goes back to the table.*

JEAN. What's in this packet?

He opens it.

What a lot of banknotes! What a lot of banknotes!

THE MOTHER. But those banknotes are no longer valid. It wasn't your father who sent them.

JEAN. It must have been Uncle Ernest. I must redeem these banknotes, they aren't worth anything any more.

THE MOTHER. Uncle Ernest doesn't make any others. You know very well that he doesn't make any others, and that he's a crook.

JEAN. I'll need a lot of money to redeem all that, more money than I have.

THE MOTHER. Well well, here's your wicked stepmother.

THE STEPMOTHER *enter, right.*

JEAN (*to the* STEPMOTHER). Madame, I need five hundred thousand francs, to redeem my Uncle Ernest, to pay my debt to my mother and her family.

THE STEPMOTHER. You're so obstinate. I've always told you to call me Hélène, not Madame.

JEAN. You know I don't like your christian name. And then, after all, you're a stranger to me.

THE STEPMOTHER. If I'm a stranger, why do you always ask me for money?

JEAN. I'll pay you back.

THE STEPMOTHER. You always say that.

JEAN. I promise you I'll pay you back this money with ten per cent interest.

Enter an OLD GENTLEMAN *who doesn't say anything, and an* OLD WOMAN.

JEAN *(to the new arrivals).* Hallo Grandmother, hallo Grandfather.

He kisses them.

Mother, why are you so old? You're as old as my grandmother and grandfather. And yet you're their daughter.

THE MOTHER. I've caught up with my parents' age. People age in the beyond, too. You get up to a hundred years old and then you stop. You'll age, too, when you've joined us.

JEAN. I'm waiting for my father; he's supposed to be coming to pay your debts.

THE GRANDMOTHER. The debt can't wait, your father still hasn't paid. We must save Ernest. He's submerged in debt. We must get him out of it.

THE STEPMOTHER. You're always coming to ask my husband for money. (*To* THE MOTHER): You aren't his wife, you aren't his wife any longer.

THE GRANDMOTHER. But Jean is his son. He has a right to a share in his father's money.

THE STEPMOTHER. He hasn't any rights at all; he's over twenty-one.

THE GRANDMOTHER (*to* THE STEPMOTHER). Even when he was a boy his father wouldn't help him. Because of you. You stopped him.
THE MOTHER (*to* THE GRANDMOTHER). Forget it, Mother, let's not talk about it any more. I'll try and find the money myself. I shall manage.
JEAN (*to* THE MOTHER). No, Mother, it's not for you to pay. I'm waiting for my father, it's up to him to come and redeem Uncle Ernest. After all, he certainly owes you that money. You know, I'm very sorry that you've aged so much since you left us all.

Enter a WOMAN.

THE WOMAN. It's because she isn't happy, there. If she was, whatever she might say, she'd look quite young. When you're happy there, time is counted backwards. It's not true when she says that you age in the beyond.
JEAN (*to* THE MOTHER). What can we do to rejuvenate you, to cheer you up?
THE GRANDMOTHER. She ought to remarry your father.
THE MOTHER. For the time being, let's at least redeem Ernest.
THE STEPMOTHER. This is my home. My house. No one's going to turn me out of it, no one's going to take my husband away from me.
THE WOMAN (*to* THE STEPMOTHER). He doesn't love you all that much. He doesn't even love you at all. At this very moment he's probably with his concubine, his mistress, the gypsy girl.
THE STEPMOTHER. You're talking nonsense, He's chosen the same family vault for him and me. He doesn't want any more to do with her.
THE MOTHER. Or with you.
THE STEPMOTHER (*to* JEAN). I'm a good Christian. I'll help you, in spite of everything. But don't try to take my husband from me. You couldn't.
THE WOMAN. Considering that he's with his gypsy girl, she's the one who's taken him from you.
THE STEPMOTHER. He's only with the gypsy girl to have a good time. But *I* understand his innermost feelings. He chose me, and it's irrevocable. (*To* JEAN). All your mother's family belong to a different species. He had to get away from them. But with me, and my brothers and my cousin —he gets on very well with us, we speak the same language. While you're waiting for your father, to prove that I'm a good Christian, here's five hundred thousand francs. I'm only giving you four hundred thousand, you must give me change.

JEAN *searches his pockets.*

JEAN. Hm, I've found a hundred thousand francs, I didn't know I had so much money left.
THE GRANDMOTHER. You ought to give us that four hundred thousand francs out of your own pocket. That's only a small proportion of the money you stole from my daughter. We shall get a little of it back.

THE MOTHER. Don't let's talk about it any more, it upsets me too much.

There is the sound of something like a telephone ringing, but there is no telephone.

THE VOICE. Hallo. Jean?
THE STEPMOTHER. Someone wants you on the telephone.
JEAN. Who is it? It's an anonymous voice that doesn't want to give a name.
THE STEPMOTHER. What are all these voices telephoning you here, as if you lived here? This is *my* house.
THE WOMAN. What you call your house has already been taken over; it belongs to everyone.
THE STEPMOTHER. Everything here belong to me, since it belongs to my husband.
JEAN. Nothing belongs to anyone. Or else, everything belongs to everyone.
THE GRANDMOTHER. Seeing that my daughter was your father's first wife, Jean, *we* have priority.
THE VOICE (*to* JEAN). Your mother, your grandfather, your grandmother, are in rags. They're all very old and very poor, they need a lot of money. And then, Ernest has to be got out of prison.
THE STEPMOTHER. They're all crooks; what a family! My husband was well advised to get rid of you.
THE GRANDMOTHER (*to* THE STEPMOTHER). Your family is no better. At least *we* didn't dispossess the peasants. We've never done anyone any harm. Your brother made a fortune out of theft, and that's why he's a top civil servant. It isn't fair, but the good Lord will know who to punish. And as for your brother, he's a murderer, he's condemned people to death. (*To* JEAN). We'll take the four hundred thousand francs, that at least is something, and we'll go away. You can join us later, we'll be waiting for you.

Exeunt THE GRANDFATHER, THE GRANDMOTHER *and* THE MOTHER. *As she goes out,* THE MOTHER *says to* JEAN:

THE MOTHER. Take care of yourself, son. And we'll be waiting for you, without much hope, but we shall always be waiting for you.
THE STEPMOTHER *(when the others have gone).* All that is just an act; it's odious. I was expecting it, but I'm a strong woman, I shan't give in, and I shall keep my husband, the house, *and* my husband's money.
THE WOMAN. That's terribly selfish; that's terribly unkind.
THE STEPMOTHER. What do I care.

She too exits.

JEAN *(lying down on the divan).* It's wonderful to be able to relax. It's good to be alive. I've got much more money than I thought I'd have. Apart from the suit I'm wearing, I have another eight. Nine, counting this one. And about a dozen pairs of shoes.
THE WOMAN. You've done some good things in your life, and you still

are. You should be pleased.

JEAN. It's so good to be able to relax.

He stands up abruptly.

THE WOMAN. Here–here's your brief-case, it's full of money. You needed me to tell you that, you didn't even know it.

JEAN. All the more reason for me to give some to the family, to Uncle Ernest. He isn't much good, but even so I can't let him rot in that hole, and anyway, I must go and find my mother, my grandmother and my grandfather. Do they still live in the rue Claude-Terrasse?

THE WOMAN. Of course they do, they've even sent us telegrams from there, they've sent us postcards.

JEAN. There aren't any through trains that go there. Do you know which bus I should take?

THE WOMAN. There's a horse-drawn carriage waiting for you outside the door.

She goes backstage and looks out.

And even a carriage and pair. Two horsepower. And another carriage with three horses.

JEAN. That would cost far too much, what with the tip you have to give the coachman, and anyway, it would take much too long to get to the other side of the town.

THE WOMAN. I'll go and look for a taxi.

JEAN. That's more modern. But you won't find one. There's no taxi rank in this neighbourhood.

THE WOMAN. I might find one in a side-street, or a cul-de-sac; people get out there, and then the drivers are free.

JEAN. The drivers won't want to go that far, this is the time they go home for their meal.

Exit THE WOMAN.

It's unlikely, very unlikely that there'd be any taxis here, everyone has a car. In the old days, there were trams.

He goes over to the table.

All these books that I don't understand. They must be books that tell you what to do when you're going to die, or when you've just died, but is all that still true? They're old books, the experiences they describe are already very ancient, *very* ancient, at any rate *I* don't understand them, I've forgotten their language. For the moment I'm rich, for the moment I'm very rich, this isn't my only house, I live in several houses, and I have several beds in each house, I sleep in a different bed every night. I don't like sleeping in the same bed.

Set. The same.

The same character is sitting in an armchair.

JEAN. What?

Pause. Enter, left, a character (JEAN 1), *who is extraordinarily like the one sitting in the armchair. Enter, right, another* CHARACTER (2) *who is just as much like the character sitting in the armchair, who doesn't move, but who seems to be the person who is speaking.*

In short, at the same time as ONE CHARACTER *enters from the left, another* CHARACTER (2), *enters from the right, who is just as similar to the* CHARACTER *in the armchair, though an older version of him. He too addresses the* CHARACTER *in the armchair. It should be immediately obvious that he is his* FATHER. *He is older, similarly dressed, but it is the* CHARACTER *who has entered from the left who answers him, not the one in the armchair.*

A way must be found to make this business immediately comprehensible. Perhaps the TWO CHARACTERS, *and especially the older one (2), should address the one in the armchair.*

CHARACTER 2 (THE FATHER). After what you said last time, I left you in peace for ages. Here you are again at last! Here you are again, in infinity! Have you got your memories back?

JEAN. I needed time!

CHARACTER 2 (THE FATHER). You ignored my wishes, and went your own way in life. I dreamed of another destiny, another career for you: a great politician, or a general, or a chemical engineer. You wouldn't listen to me. I know—and I don't hold it against her any longer—that it was your mother who pushed you into other directions.

JEAN. You *do* still hold it against her! You'll hold it against her for all eternity. And so long as you do, you won't go to heaven. I came here, I'm sitting in this chair, in order to answer your questions.

CHARACTER 2 (THE FATHER). Don't go on at me! I have to admit that you've made a fine career for yourself, you've succeeded in life, but is that going to be any good to you here? If only it were possible, we ought to start all over again. Start again! But, well, you've been a tremendous success, President of the Academy, founder of a literary school, opposed by a lot of adversaries.

JEAN. You can't please everyone. And it's hard to please your father. You always have more opponents than sycophants. But I've had some good people on my side. The greatest critics, the greatest professors of aesthetics. I've built monuments of literature and poetry. None of my contemporaries was greater than I.

When I was a schoolboy, you used to go into my room. You searched my drawers. You looked through my exercise books; all you found in them were caricatures, instead of the homework my teachers had set me. You made me go over everything I was supposed to have learnt, you made me recite it all to you, I couldn't remember a word, and yet I passed all my exams, I got all the degrees I sat for. Because *they* understood that I was a genius, they realised that even though my father was ashamed of me, even though you were ashamed of me and locked me in my room and hid all my books, even though you burnt my Dostoevskys and my Kafkas, my Flauberts and my Kierkegaards, I myself was a Flaubert and a Kierkegaard.

You slapped my face, you beat me, but my teachers never minded when I got nought in mathematics, they believed in me, and they used to lend me their own copies of the authors you threw into the fire, and they allowed me to read Racine and Shakespeare during the physics lessons. The physics teachers pretended not to notice. I'm settling my accounts with you now, and what I reproach you for is that you tried to stop me doing so many things. You were a blind paterfamilias.

You made me have private coaching in chemistry at home, to pass the exam to become a chemical engineer, but my coach secretly brought me the forbidden books, and reproductions of Leonardo's *Last Supper*. I ran away from home and found friends who helped me, I discovered drink, which I liked, and girls, whom I adored!

All through my adolescence you kept me in confinement, but you couldn't get the better of me. I was the stronger, I was stronger than you.

CHARACTER 2 (THE FATHER). Yes, my son. And mostly, you went to your mother. She encouraged you to rebel against me. She wasn't one of us. That was why we didn't get on. She must be dead too, now, somewhere.

JEAN. She was proud of my victory over you. But she was especially proud of my success. I was right.

CHARACTER 2 (THE FATHER). Yes, it's true, I have to admit it, you did achieve glory. You were famous among the living. I mean: among the dying—do the dead remember you? They know as little about you as they would have if you'd only been a modest chemical engineer. Yes, yes, I can't deny it, I didn't believe you'd succeed, I didn't believe in your intelligence. You belong to your mother's race, not to mine.

JEAN. You were brutal and you were violent, you used to beat your servants and browbeat your employees.

CHARACTER 2 (THE FATHER). They're all dead now, and they remember neither your great deeds nor my brutality. There's no difference between a bastard and a genius. No, though; I ought to repent.

JEAN. You ought to repent!

CHARACTER 2 (THE FATHER). I ought to repent! But was my discipline worse than the madness you put into people's heads? Neither of them counts any more. No one is a brute for all eternity. Eternity is the great leveller. No no, son, no no. I'm talking rubbish, I'm simply trying to justify myself. You've won. I don't know exactly what you've won, but it's quite certain that you were highly thought of by the most influential people. I've seen your works in bookshops and libraries.

I haven't read any of them; everything I know about you is just hearsay. Gossip and rumours, gossip, gossip. Now that we have time, show me what you've done, let me know a bit about it; that'll make my defeat even more crushing, and I'll be able to appreciate your glory, and know why I should admire you.

JEAN. I'll show it to you. It's in my drawers, as it was when I was a child.

CHARACTER 2 (THE FATHER). Show me! Show me, son!

There is a table in the front of the stage. The CHARACTER *in the armchair stands up, goes over to the table and opens a drawer, then a second, then a third.*

JEAN. Here you are, then.

He takes some yellowed paper out of the drawers, and some tattered old exercise books which fall on to the ground. He picks up a few pages.

The FATHER *stands and contemplates all this with an expressionless face.*

JEAN *then brings out some bits of rusty wire, a cookery book, some bad caricatures, some dirty bits of rag, some unsharpened pencils, and a bottle of ink, which spills on to the stage.*

There; that's everything I've done.

CHARACTER 2 (THE FATHER). All that stuff is what you had in your drawers when you were a child.

JEAN. Nothing else? That's all there is, I must have left some things somewhere, that's all!

CHARACTER 2 (THE FATHER). That's all?

JEAN. That's all! But I oughtn't to have sweated my guts out for that. Yes, Father, that *is* all. Where are my monuments? Where is my glory?

He opens a fourth drawer and takes out handfuls of dust.

Here! Here! Is this better than nothing?

CHARACTER 2 (THE FATHER). And that's your complete works?

JEAN. Everything has to be rethought. Everything has to be begun again.

He sits down in the chair again.

But I shall continue to defend the Occident, the venerability of the Greek cosmos, the liberty conferred on us by the planets, by Existentialism and Gnosticism, the right to make inferences, Valentinian speculation, The Song of the Pearl. The defence of the Occident, the dance of the stimulant, the defence of the Occident, the Occident of defence, the March on Rome, the Invasion of Tuscany, the tusks of the elephant, his tusks are his defence, the tusker's defence, the defence of the Occident, the defence of the occiput, and of my political itinerary. The Rights of Man, the state of culture, the cults of the Orient, the defence of the Occident, the elephant's tusk, the Tuscan's elephant. Hannibal . . .

He collapses.

Set. A shabby, rather sordid flat.
Characters. The FILM-MAKER, JEAN, *the* GRANDMOTHER, *etc.*

THE OLD WOMAN. Jean, Jean!

Enter JEAN, *from the back.*

JEAN. Yes, Madame, here I am!
THE OLD WOMAN. I am not Madame, I'm your grandmother. You never know whether I'm your grandmother or the old concierge; you're always mixing us up.
JEAN. I'm sorry—I have so many worries. My head's bursting with them.
THE OLD WOMAN. What about me, then! At my age! What am I supposed to say?
JEAN. There's nothing to stop a grandmother being a concierge.
THE OLD WOMAN. The producer you were expecting, the film-maker, he's here, he's come with a proposition. Fix your hair a bit, and your tie. He's offering you twenty per cent of the profits.

She disappears.

Enter, right, the FILM-MAKER.

THE FILM-MAKER. Write the script for me, and I'll give you twenty per cent of the receipts. With an advance.
JEAN. You could give me half right away. I'm still capable of getting an interesting idea, you know; I have a lot of interesting ideas. I'm not all that old, they must have told you, and anyway, it's obvious. So long as you go on dreaming, you stay young. You must excuse this shabby flat. In the old days, when I lived here with my wife and daughter, it was in a much better state. I only come back from time to time, and usually on my own, but I can assure you I don't actually live in this gloomy ground floor. My family is in the country, now, I'm just here for a few days, but I don't *live* in this dismal place. I'm not broke. I'm still sitting pretty, sitting very pretty indeed. My big flat in the rue de Pathé is much bigger, but I've got the builders in, there, which is why I'm here, and why I arranged to meet you here. I have to be in Paris from time to time because I also own a huge house in the country, but it's too far away even by car. My country house is an enormous castle, a palace, it has innumerable rooms, a whole lot of salons full of antique furniture. I also have a more modern salon, it's vast, I have unlimited space. I've turned some of the attics into a theatre, with a proper stage and a special entrance for the actors, and I have still other attics where I grow trees. I shall have to prune them a little when they reach the ceiling. They're quite tall enough as it is. There's an artificial lake in my attic, but I still have a vast amount of space waiting to be developed. There are meadows that I haven't enough money left to do anything with. I need millions upon millions, maybe I shall earn millions with this script. There's no need to get a designer for our sets, the palace itself provides the decor. There are enough stages, enough studios to shoot anything you like in, but I must earn some money from the script. If I provide the decors and the

location, maybe you could give me thirty per cent, forty per cent, fifty per cent? Well yes, I have to keep my palaces in repair, some of the castles in my palace will go to rack and ruin if I don't look after them. There are real ruins, too, but they musn't be touched, they're meant to be ruins. You know what I mean. Let's sign the contract.

THE FILM-MAKER. What sort of script are you going to write for me?

JEAN. In the first place, the description. It's a whole film in itself, just waiting to be made. All the spaces, the walls, the furniture, the dozens of lakes. No need for location shots, because all the outdoor locations are indoors. We won't have to worry about the weather.

THE FILM-MAKER. Right, that's the ambience—but where's the action?

Enter THE OLD WOMAN.

THE OLD WOMAN. I've just arrived from Foreign Parts, I had a good trip, but it was tiring.

JEAN. How nice to see you, Grandmother.

THE OLD WOMAN. Are you sure I'm your grandmother?

JEAN. Yes! Quite sure. (*To* THE FILM-MAKER). Excuse me, sir, I'm not sure whether this woman is my grandmother or my mother. If she's my mother, she's aged a lot. (*To* THE WOMAN). Are you my mother?

THE OLD WOMAN. I'm still waiting for the money, my money that I left with your father. I'm still waiting. You promised me you'd ask him. He owes it to me! Don't you dare go there?—Are you afraid of him? I've aged, while I was waiting. I've come back yet again from Foreign Parts, hoping he'll give it to me. When you think that he's made millions!

JEAN (*to* THE FILM-MAKER). She's my mother, sir—you know what I mean.

THE OLD WOMAN. And yet we had some very enjoyable times. I was a bit damp there, because the cellar is directly underneath. But when we had some coal, and all the doors and windows were closed, it wasn't at all bad. I like dark old houses. We enjoyed being with your wife and daughter, it was like being in a nest.

JEAN. How can she have aged so terribly? There *is* an explanation: she's waiting for the money from my father. That isn't an adequate explanation. (*To* THE FILM-MAKER). You're staying somewhere near here?

THE FILM-MAKER. It's quite close. At an hotel, le Capitole, not la Coupole, le Capitole. At the Porte de Saint-Cloud, a luxury hotel. I live in luxury hotels.

JEAN. It's very new, very modern, it must have been built very quickly, I didn't know it.

THE FILM-MAKER. I have no permanent address.

THE OLD WOMAN (*to* JEAN). When the gentleman has gone, come and see me in my concierge's lodge.

She goes out.

THE FILM-MAKER. I like living in different places, going from one hotel to another, from one town to another, in different countries. It's only two or three streets to my hotel—very old, very beautiful streets.

The backdrop changes: streets and gardens pass by.

JEAN *(suddenly very happy).* It's so green, so beautiful, so sunny! The colours, the light!

For a few more moments the landscape in the background keeps moving, showing beautiful houses and gardens, which JEAN *contemplates in silence. Pause.*

THE FILM-MAKER. You see!

Then, still in the background, other streets appear, which become less and less beautiful, anonymous, dirty. The bright light has disappeared.

JEAN. What an anticlimax. Anonymous suburbs again. And they aren't even slums, they're just anonymous. That square, the Porte de Saint-Cloud, isn't very far away, but it's difficult to get to because of the traffic, there aren't any taxis or buses.

Both start walking on the stage as if they were walking in the street.

If it is found to be impracticable to show this scene, it can simply be suggested, first by a strong light, and then by a grey light.

Ah! the luxury hotel!

And in fact, the picture of a luxury hotel appears in the background.

The decor changes: the stage is divided into two. On the left, a luxurious, but tasteless room. On the other side of the partition dividing the stage, three or four dirty beds, with people in uniform lying on them.

THE FILM-MAKER. That's my room.

JEAN. And on the other side?

THE FILM-MAKER: Why are you so surprised? There aren't any really private rooms in the hotels they build these days, you're only separated from the other guests by a sort of semi-partition. But the people who live there don't make any noise. For the moment, they're N.C.O.s. You can't ever be alone any more; at the very most, you can have a cubicle in a little corner of the dormitory. That's to stop spies getting in.

Enter, left a hotel PAGE-BOY, *carrying a suitcase.*

THE PAGE-BOY. Here you are, sir.

Exit.

JEAN. Do you still get your suitcase brought up by a page-boy? That's extraordinary!

THE FILM-MAKER. It's one of the rare privileges film-makers still enjoy, among others, but it *is* rare. I must leave you.

JEAN. I used to travel alone a lot, too, in the old days, from hotel to hotel, with no fixed address, either, in the south of France, in Italy, the Italy of the old days; in Spain, royalist Spain.

The bedcover falls off, and discloses a woman lying in the bed.

THE FILM-MAKER. Careful!
JEAN: How white she is!
THE FILM-MAKER. Careful; you mustn't touch her. All you may do is smell her, and look at her breasts. I'll leave you.

Exit THE FILM-MAKER. *Enter a* FAT MAN.

THE FAT MAN. Young man, contemplation is preferable to possession.

Enter a LADY.

THE LADY. I've just arrived. I've been away for a long time and you didn't even come to meet me at the station. I sent you a telegram, though. You forget everything!
JEAN. I'm afraid that's true; I forget everything.
THE LADY. One fine day you'll forget to put your socks on, and you'll go out into the street barefoot.
JEAN. And yet you had a good journey!
THE LADY. I had a good journey! Mountains, sky, sea, lakes in the sky, sky in the water, freshwater rivers.

Set: Ground floor in the rue Claude-Terrasse, which turns into the mill in La Chapelle-Anthenaise, and is then transformed into a huge manor house, like the one at Cerisy-la-Salle.

JEAN. How is it that she isn't here? I happened to be passing through this district, and I've come to see my mother. I haven't written to her for a long time, and I haven't seen her for a long time, either. But she has written to me. She was here quite recently.
THE OTHER MAN. I don't know who you're talking about. When we rented this flat it was empty. There was no one in it.
JEAN. Where can she be now? She has nowhere to live, poor woman!
A WOMAN: You can leave tomorrow morning. You can sleep here tonight.
JEAN. I don't want to sleep in a room occupied by someone else.
THE WOMAN: But there are two beds, there are even three. You won't have to share your bed.
JEAN. At the manor house, at Cerisy, I got into bad habits, as you might say. Everyone had his own room.
THE WOMAN: Not in your old mill, in La Chapelle-Anthenaise.
JEAN. That's just it: the mill was here.
THE WOMAN: Here, in our flat?
JEAN. Yes, here. In this very place. In my day it was inhabited by the Loisnards: Marie; her father, Baptiste; her mother, Jeannette. Haven't you ever heard of those people? Who did you buy the mill from?

THE WOMAN. It was abandoned when we found it, we restored it, everything had to be repaired. If there are a lot of people to each room, it's because there are a lot of us working here; we don't live like lords.

JEAN. We didn't live like lords in my day, either, not in the mill. At Cerisy, though, it wasn't the same thing; there, people lived like lords of the manor. I'm not altogether reassured yet, though I realize that my fear was exaggerated. And to think that I have been so terribly frightened for nearly a century, eh, getting on for a century. For almost a century I didn't know where I'd come from. I didn't know where I was going, I didn't know where I was. And then, since the unusual had become the usual, and abnormality had become the norm, I told myself that even so, I *was* perhaps at home. No no, not all the time. Just sometimes, by fits and starts. All the same, though, I did take dreams for reality, I was caught up in the machinery. I had a profession which I took to be a vocation. I functioned, in order to forget my fear. Oh yes, I did feel at home, as from a certain moment. There were forms, there were objects in space, and then the objects suddenly took on monstrous forms, to remind me, no doubt, that I was *not* at home. Where was I, then? The chair was a dragon with two heads, and the wardrobe was something that looked like a lake. A strange sort of lake: where did it come from?

THE WOMAN. Well, here too you have only one chair, which is only a chair, and a table. You can put your hand on the table, it's solid. Touch it.

JEAN. That's true, it really is a chair, but it isn't like the one I knew there, is it a transfigured chair? A model chair? An archetypal chair? It was in the other place that the chairs were fakes, they were the ghosts of chairs, that must be why they took on a frightening, or incredible, or monstrous appearance. I was so terribly afraid of the black void, of the dark tunnel I might have plunged into and fallen into the bottomless pit. But it wasn't that at all, it didn't turn out to be that, I can't believe my eyes, this is a real chair, a quintessential chair, and this table is a quintessential table. You can feel that all these things are real. Their very presence is enough to make you believe in their eternity, in reality. In the other place, presences seemed to be nothing but appearances. I am much more at my ease here. In the midst of truth. But is it truly true? Certainly, you feel better, I feel better, but is that really what it is?

THE WOMAN. Yes, it's more or less that.

JEAN. It's still an approximation, then? Why the 'more or less'?

THE WOMAN. Try and keep calm; then you'll gradually be able to get your wits together again.

JEAN. And yet this isn't a bit like a clinic; you don't have clinics here, do you? It's quite certain that I'm in another place. I can only keep repeating just how amazed and delighted I am that it could all happen so well, that there wasn't any dark abyss, any bottomless gulf. There was no moment when I felt terrified that I was going to fall. I simply took one step, and an invisible door opened. I've travelled hundreds of kilometres through the world, thousands of kilometres, but now, to come here, a door half-opened, or else I came through a window or through a looking-glass. I wasn't even aware that it was happening. And it's the longest journey. But you tell me that this world is only approximately real, only more or less real; where is the real one, then, the completely real one?

THE WOMAN. You're already feeling the pure air of the completely real, here. And yet this is only the antechamber to the real, which doesn't move. I have to lead you farther. Don't be afraid, it isn't measurable, it's neither long nor short, but I have to take you there with some other people.

JEAN. I thought as much; I know who I have to meet, don't I?

THE WOMAN. Yes, you do.

THE WOMAN *is the owner of the house; she should look like a farmers wife.*

Characters: Two women: perhaps MADAME SIMPSON, *Jean's stepmother, and* ARLETTE, *Jean's wife, and perhaps sometimes his sister.*

MADAME SIMPSON or THE FIRST WOMAN. There's no denying it, it never stops moving!

ARLETTE or THE SECOND WOMAN: We've got ourselves into a hell of a hornets' nest!

She laughs.

MADAME SIMPSON. If only my husband's family weren't here!

ARLETTE. We're in a fine mess! If anyone had asked my opinion, I wouldn't have agreed.

MADAME SIMPSON. It never stops moving, but at the same time it doesn't budge!

ARLETTE. It's moving! If only it would stop moving. And all the time the same movements, the same movements cyclically!

MADAME SIMPSON. When I'm dead! Oh my God!

ARLETTE. I'm always expecting a catastrophe, I wonder how long it can hold up. What if the earth were to crack!

MADAME SIMPSON. I can hear them, I'm watching them. They're gesticulating, they're talking, too, I think; I can't understand them.

ARELETTE. Where would we go if the earth were to crack? Down the hole! We'll go down the hole before the earth cracks.

MADAME SIMPSON. Scientists, judges, field officers, have told me that the moon might come closer to us and get stuck to the earth.

ARLETTE. It'd more likely be us who'd go and enlarge the moon!

MADAME SIMPSON. It gives me the cold shivers, just to think about it. Where can we hide, my dear? Where would we go?

ARLETTE. There's plenty of room in the Russian steppes, in Siberia.

MADAME SIMPSON. For us?

ARLETTE. For the moon.

MADAME SIMPSON. Three quarters of a century ago a great big stone, a whole mountain, fell out of the sky on to Siberia, it made a big hole, but the earth held up.

ARLETTE. No one in Europe heard anything.

MADAME SIMPSON. Oh yes they did, it made a noise like thunder, people thought it was thunder.

ARLETTE. There was no mention of it in the press!

MADAME SIMPSON. My grandmother's mother heard about it, but it was soon censored, not a word in the papers.

ARLETTE. Whose interests was it in to hide it from us?

MADAME SIMPSON. Maybe the devil's!

ARLETTE. Maybe God's!

MADAME SIMPSON. They may well have come to an understanding–made a treaty.

ARLETTE. We can't possibly know. It's pure supposition.

MADAME SIMPSON. There's the earth, there are the planets, there are the stars; where does it all end?

ARLETTE. We must do what our poodle does. He doesn't ask himself that question.

MADAME SIMPSON. Live like a poodle!

ARLETTE. It all goes up to heaven.

MADAME SIMPSON. And heaven comes down to us again. It surrounds us.

ARLETTE. Does heaven come after the stars, beyond them, or is it between the stars?

MADAME SIMPSON. It must be a completely different world. It really is elsewhere.

ARLETTE. It must be a bigger world than ours, to be able to hold everything.

MADAME SIMPSON. It gives me the shivers all over again when I think about it, it's all so mysterious!

ARLETTE. Who is the Father of God?

MADAME SIMPSON. I haven't the slightest idea; not the slightest.

ARLETTE. It seems that life wouldn't be possible if there weren't any mysteries, and shivers, and anguish, and fear.

MADAME SIMPSON. God is great, but greater than what? I say 'My God', but I don't know who he is.

ARLETTE. Maybe he's Matter–but then, we don't know what Matter is, either.

MADAME SIMPSON. If I were in that hole I wouldn't be asking myself these questions any more, but shall I still be shivering when I'm in the cold of the earth?

ARLETTE. Some graves are kept in very good condition.

MADAME SIMPSON. You need to have children who love you and who look after them. But I shall have an heiress, she'll say Masses, and bring flowers.

ARLETTE. An heiress! With my father-in-law's money?

MADAME SIMPSON. I have every right to it, he's my husband.

ARLETTE. I don't know whether Jean and the law will agree.
MADAME SIMPSON. My husband is above the law, he twists the law round his little finger.
ARLETTE: No one is stronger than the law.
MADAME SIMPSON. Unless they change it. They'll change it.
ARLETTE: You're so selfish. Who will look after Jean's grave?
MADAME SIMPSON. He has his children. From children to children, that's the way it goes, until the end of the world. Afterwards, all the tombs will be opened. Then there won't be any point in caring for them.
ARLETTE. Some tombs are a thousand years old but they still seem quite new. Some are only six months old, but they're already much the worse for wear.
MADAME SIMPSON. You see, from inheritance to inheritance, we can go on until the end.
ARLETTE. You have no right to that inheritance.
MADAME SIMPSON. Why do you want to deprive me of that sort of immortality?
ARLETTE. Why do you want to deprive other people of it?
MADAME SIMPSON. It's a fight, it's the struggle for life. I shall fight.
ARLETTE. We shall fight too, with all our might, and anyway, how vain you are! Comets' tails could hit the tombs and smash them to smithereens, with all their contents.
MADAME SIMPSON. They could also carry them up to outer space.
ARLETTE. I won't let that happen to you. Jean and I will prevent it.
MADAME SIMPSON. We shall see who is the stronger!
ARLETTE. I shall stop you!
MADAME SIMPSON. You won't be able to.
ARLETTE. You start talking about the great problems of life, of the world, of heaven, only to end up with some pettifogging story about an inheritance. You're petty! And you're stupid.
MADAME SIMPSON. And you're just a bastard! An illegitimate child!
ARLETTE. You're a liar, a hypocrite, and a fool.
MADAME SIMPSON. I won't let you get away with it.
ARLETTE. Jean and I won't let *you* get away with it!

Exit MADAME SIMPSON.

ARLETTE (*alone*). No, we won't let her get away with it! Is it all true? With Jean, who lets everything go by default, because he's tired, or sceptical, it's not so sure! When the entire earth is covered in cemeteries, where'll they put the rest of the dead? They'll have to burn them. But that'll make too much ash. Where will they put the ashes?

Set: A bus stop.

A LADY. It's still not here, but it's a nice day, you don't mind waiting.
AN OLD FELLOW. Just as well I brought my umbrella, what with this never-ending rain.
JEAN. What a wonderful day!
AN OLD MAN. I'm completely resigned.
SECOND OLD MAN. I can't bring myself to become resigned.
A LADY. The young aren't any happier than we are.
JEAN. I love this town, with the Seine flowing into the Thames.
THE OLD GENTLEMAN. Have they finally built the canal?
SECOND OLD MAN. I was the one who struck the first blow with the pickaxe, seventy years ago. They still haven't finished the canal, but the waters merge, on account of the pollution.
AN OLD LADY. Pollution is what makes it possible for us to live, but just look at that cloud, it's the clouds that transport the waters of the Seine into the Thames.
THE OTHER LADY. And vice and versa.
A LADY. I like buses that look like underground trains.
THE OTHER LADY. When you think what men have done, eh! They didn't do half as much when they lived in caves.
A LADY. They weren't nearly so well educated in those days. There was no compulsory schooling.
THE OLD MAN. Compulsory or not, it doesn't make much difference.
JEAN. We're surround by woods, lakes, mountains. What a wonderful day!
AN OLD FELLOW. What a terrible squall, and they've broken my umbrella.
A LADY. Here–take my parasol, instead of your umbrella. That'll improve the weather.
THE OLD MAN. I like the rain!
JEAN: Really, what wonderful weather! It makes you feel like singing.

He sings.

A LADY *(having listened to the song).* Once you've started you never stop, you deafen me, my husband has a lute, too.
THE OTHER LADY. But it still doesn't make the tram come.
JEAN. It isn't a tram, it's a bus–full of pretty ladies and flowers.
THE OLD MAN. I'm resigned to everything . . . I'm a true patriot.
SECOND OLD MAN. I shall never become resigned, the temptations of old age are even worse than the temptations of youth.
THE LADY. That's true, too.
THE OTHER LADY. Everything is contained in everything, and vice and versa.
JEAN. Do you know 'The Song of the Private Individual'?
THE OLD MAN. I used to know 'The Song of the Private Soldier'.
THE OTHER LADY. They're more or less much the same.

A MAIDEN LADY *(entering very quickly):* I conquered, I saw, I came!
THE OLD FELLOW. The weather's changed since you gave me your sunshade, it's fine now, but that doesn't make the tram come, nor even the bus, as you call it.
THE LADY. The more ye seek, the less ye find.
JEAN. I have more than one string to my bow.
THE OLD FELLOW *(to* THE YOUNG MAN*)*: I've lost all my strings *and* my bow.
THE LADY. There's a rainbow.
THE OTHER LADY. If the cost of living didn't keep going up, and if wages were increased, we'd certainly have more cash in the till.
THE OLD FELLOW. Till the State came and took it away from us.
JEAN: Man comes and tills the fields, but I till the till. I put my hand in it, there's nothing in it, but I still have some savings.
THE OLD FELLOW. I knew an old Japanese, when I was young; he had neither stirngs nor bow, but even so he drew a bow at a venture.
THE OLD MAN. I sell bows, and arrows, and plates, but people only buy them in order to break them, so that comes even more expensive.
THE LADY. Ever since I gave him my sunshade, it's been raining.
THE OLD FELLOW. Ever since I've had the sunshade the sun's been shining, but the sun gets in my eyes, that's because the sunshade has a hole in it.
THE OLD MAN. Well, all you have to do to plug the holes is put other holes in the holes.
SECOND OLD MAN. The State's made up of men who are in a sorry state.
THE MAIDEN LADY. A sorry State is better than a sorry sire.
THE LADY. Sires are the husbands of sirens.
JEAN. That's not true; wave corpuscles have made a lot of progress since then.
THE MAIDEN LADY. Are you a determinist of an indeterminist?
JEAN. Personally, I prefer beauty. So long as the weather is beautiful, and towns are beautiful, and wave mechanics is decked out with chrysanthemums, I'm not bored with life.
EACH CHARACTER, ONE AFTER THE OTHER: Here's the bus, here's the bus.
THE OLD FELLOW. This one took its time, too. That's no way to prolong the years of life.

They all rush into the bus, which crosses the stage and disappears into the wings on the other side, right.

THE MAIDEN LADY *(clapping her hands).* It's a real bus, it's a real bus, it'll take us to see unknown lands.
THE OLD FELLOW. There aren't any unknown lands left, not since they discovered the North Pole.
THE LADY. There are other North Poles.

THE OLD MAN: Those are the North Poles of other manifestations of divinity, I know them all, and what I say unto you, is: Shit.

THE MAIDEN LADY. There's no need to be vulgar. I was brought up according to other principles. I haven't killed anyone yet.

JEAN *may be among these characters, or there may instead be another young character who has nothing to do with anyone.*

Set: A modest, rather dark room. In the back wall, two windows giving on to the street. Silhouettes pass by. In the room, two mattresses on the floor, a chair, a table, an old armchair, a rocking-chair. A very old woman, in the rocking-chair, is mending socks. The character can be seen passing the windows. After a moment there is a knock at the door.

THE OLD WOMAN. Who's there?

JEAN. It's me, Jean, your son.

THE OLD WOMAN. We weren't expecting him any more. Come in.

JEAN *opens the door.*

You took your time making up your mind to come.

JEAN. Hallo, Mother.

THE OLD WOMAN. It's such a long time since we saw each other. I'm not your mother, I'm your maternal grandmother.

JEAN. Is my mother still alive?

THE OLD WOMAN: Yes. She's at work. We've been back in Paris for two years. Your mother and I weren't expecting you any more, she'd given you up.

JEAN. There are still some fine old houses with little gardens in your district. I can plead extenuating circumstances; I've tried to come several times. I was in the street, on my way to see you. And then, the street was only a cul-de-sac, I had to go back the way I came. I made detours, I crossed other streets, but they were all cul-de-sacs. I've tried to come at least twenty times. There was always a house or a fence blocking my way, so I'd give up and start again another day, but it was always the same: cul-de-sacs, railings, very high fences. But this time I've managed to find you. I made a detour, then I came to a gateway, I went through it, and discovered that it led to a passage that quite simply came out into your street. I don't know whether I'll be able to find the passage and the gateway again when I want to go home, perhaps I could sleep here? But I've always been afraid of never seeing my mother alive again. I recognize you now, you're my grandmother.

THE OLD WOMAN. We've been waiting for you long enough.

JEAN. Yes. What do you live on? I've come to bring you some provisions. Here's a whole sackful.

He takes the sack off his back and puts it on the ground.

Look, I've got fruit, I've got vegetables, I've got flowers.
THE OLD WOMAN. Your mother has found work in a factory. And I'm the concierge in this house. You see, we made our own way without your help.

Enter THE MOTHER.

JEAN. Mother, Mother, why do you look so indifferent at the sight of me?
THE MOTHER. Is it you? I'd given you up!
THE OLD WOMAN. After all, your mother has been here in the same town as you for nearly two years, it's almost two years. Almost in the same district, and you never came, even though I sent you a telegram.
THE MOTHER. I waited and waited, and then I became reconciled to it.
JEAN *(to* THE MOTHER*)*. How you've changed, how thin you've got, you're as thin as a rake! The reason I didn't come before was that I had to finish my studies. I'm twenty-nine, and I still haven't got my degree. I would so much have liked to come and show you my diploma, but then I decided to come without it. But, as I told you, I couldn't find the street.
THE MOTHER. You lived here when you were little, though.

A silhouette can be seen passing on the other side of the window, and almost immediately there is a knock at the door.

JEAN. That must be my father.
THE GRANDMOTHER: He's never been here.
THE MOTHER. Since he remarried he doesn't come to see us, either. He's afraid of his wife.

The door opens. Enters a MAN *of fifty-five.*

THE FATHER (*to the* TWO WOMEN). It's your fault that he hasn't completed his studies. He was always thinking about you. He never thought about anything else.
THE GRANDMOTHER (*to the* MAN). *You* stopped him coming.
THE MOTHER. It isn't our fault that we're still alive. You can keep your son, now.
THE FATHER. He's crazy, he has ridiculous blanks. He passed the first exams for his degree, and the last ones. But he failed the ones in the middle, that's his big gap.

Enter, by another door, on the audience's right, THE SISTER, *who seems almost as old as* THE MOTHER.

THE MOTHER (*to* JEAN). Here's your sister.
THE SISTER. My mother keeps us, me and Grandmother. (*To* THE FATHER). Neither you nor Jean have ever sent us a sou.
THE FATHER. That was because I was very disappointed by Jean's gaps.
THE MOTHER (*to* JEAN). Your grandmother must have told you: You can live here, if you can't live with your father any longer. You know the flat.
JEAN. I've already seen it in a dream.

THE MOTHER (*to* JEAN). There's a room for you on the first floor.
THE SISTER. You go up the wooden stairs, there's a room there that you know so well, the very long, dark one near mine, it isn't very comfortable.
JEAN. I know; it only has a tiny little skylight at the far end. But even so, I'm glad to have somewhere to stay.
THE GRANDMOTHER. While you're waiting to finish your studies, and be able to marry and have somewhere better to live.
THE FATHER. He's a good-for-nothing, he'll never make a proper career for himself, he'll never be a barrister like me.
JEAN. It's my fault, it's my fault, I know that at my age, I'll soon be thirty, I ought to have finished my studies, but I don't think I'm going to be able to, I can't put my mind on them. The only thing that interests me is the theatre.
THE FATHER. I shan't give you another sou.
THE GRANDMOTHER (*to* JEAN). Your mother will have to go on working, and wearing herself out, but she won't be able to do that all her life.
JEAN. I can't be any help to her at the moment, though.
THE GRANDMOTHER (*to* JEAN). You'll never be any help to her.
JEAN. What can I do, what can I do.

He wrings his hands.

THE GRANDMOTHER. He feels guilty, but that won't get us anywhere.
THE SISTER. It's your nature to sponge on other people.
THE FATHER. Keep him here with you, if you like.

Set: A large room. On one side, a petit bourgeois living room: three armchairs, a settee, a little table, oil lamp on the table. At the back, an old-fashioned fireplace and a large mirror. All this is stage left. Stage right: a kind of dormitory with four camp-beds.

Lying on the settee, a WOMAN *of about forty-five, wearing a black dress and a big necklace. She is rather beautiful, and only slightly common. On the two stools, facing* MARGUERITE SIMPSON. JEAN SIMPSON*—a youngish man—and* LYDIA.

MADAME SIMPSON. So here you are at last, Jean. I knew you'd come back to Pamplona. You don't despise us any more, then, because you need money. Your father has sent you money regularly, an enormous amount.
JEAN. He's my father, Madame Simpson. It's perfectly natural. If I fell out with him, it was because of you, Madame Simpson.
MADAME SIMPSON. You never wanted to call me Aunt Marguerite.
JEAN. You aren't the sister of either of my parents.
MADAME SIMPSON. You didn't want to call me Aunt. That's what people call their father's second wife. I didn't ask you to call me Mother, but I didn't want you to call me Madame Simpson.

JEAN. That was no reason to get people—and me too—to think that my mother, my real mother, was dead.

MADAME SIMPSON. It was your father who wanted everyone to think that, even me, and especially me, so he could marry me. My brothers, the two Captains, were quite willing for me to marry a widower, but not a divorced man. I never really believed in your mother's death, though. Is she still alive?

JEAN. You ought to know. When I left her she was living in Pamplona. I wrote to her, the war broke out, I've had no news of her since. So I'm asking you to tell me the truth. Is she still alive, or not?

MADAME SIMPSON. I caught a glimpse of her some years ago. Who knows what became of her. She used to live in a poor neighbourhood, a low-built house, just one dark, damp room.

JEAN. A slum, obviously. Whereas you lived in a palace. It's a small town, you might have met her by chance when you where out for a walk.

MADAME SIMPSON: It was your father who didn't want anything to do with her.

JEAN. You did everything you could to see that he didn't. My father was the Chief of Police . . .

MADAME SIMPSON: He still is!

JEAN. He could have had some enquiries made. In any case, I've come to fetch her, if she's still alive, and to take her to Paris to live with me.

MADAME SIMPSON. You say you adore her, yet you tell me you've stopped writing to her. You shouldn't have dropped her.

JEAN. There was the war.

MADAME SIMPSON. It only lasted for a time.

JEAN. I know. I didn't altogether do what I should have done. I'm not ungrateful, I'm neglectful. Asthenic.

MADAME SIMPSON. You've always accused me of being the cause of your misfortunes. There was nothing I could do to go against your father's wishes.

JEAN. You brought out his worst side.

MADAME SIMPSON. Who is that woman with you?

JEAN. She's Lydia.

LYDIA. I'm Lydia.

MADAME SIMPSON. You're the one who ran away from home when you were fourteen, with a bundle on your back. I had no alternative but to turn you out. You used to sleep in the same room as your father and me. You came between us. You spied on us, and prevented any intimacy between my husband and me. Or maybe you aren't Lydia? Perhaps you're the other one, Jean's wife? In that case you'll remember that it was I and my husband who put your engagement ring on your finger.

Turning to THE YOUNG MAN.

Is she your sister or your wife? (*to* LYDIA). Jean made a good marriage, a good choice. Alas. Afterwards, there was the war, and all those separations, so we don't recognize each other any more. (*To* JEAN).

It wasn't my business to get in touch with your mother; I am your father's legal wife.

JEAN. My mother was that before you. You used to say that my sister and I were bastards, you don't know the meaning of words.

MADAME SIMPSON. I don't hang about in the streets, for goodness' sake, I don't go ferreting around in every district. I have to lie down most of the time, I get stomach aches, I have constipation.

JEAN. You'll die of it! If only you would die of it!

MADAME SIMPSON (*to* JEAN). What happened in the years before the war, in the war years, in the years after the war?

JEAN. Before the war, as you know, I was banished. Luckily I was able to escape to that golden country which welcomed us so warmly, which adopted us.

LYDIA (*to* JEAN). I'm grateful to that nation. No one must say anything against it. What would have become of us?

JEAN. At the beginning of the war I was in the army. Later, they discharged me, they replaced me. After that I worked in a shipyard for the Ottoman navy, but I didn't become a Turkish citizen.

MADAME SIMPSON. You came here to your father's house, to our house, not to be friendly but to challenge me–or perhaps you came to enquire after my health? You want to know whether I'm going to die soon. There's nothing wrong with me, apart from my constipation, but that isn't serious. You aren't going to come into your inheritance just yet. And in any case, it's all been put in my name, I have the disposal of everything, the house is me, the money is me. You and your sister or your wife will get nothing. Your father gives you enough money while he's alive.

JEAN. I simply came to look for my mother.

LYDIA. If Father gave him any money, it was behind your back, because you wouldn't have allowed it.

MADAME SIMPSON. That's not true, he doesn't hide anything from me. *I* told him to give you some money.

JEAN. He only sends me money when I'm rich and famous. When I'm down and out he turns his back on me. He's ashamed.

MADAME SIMPSON. He couldn't have sent you any money during the war, there was no way of getting letters through the enemy lines. And in any case, it wasn't worth anything. What with the inflation.

JEAN. You haven't anything for us to eat. I don't know why I'm so hungry.

MADAME SIMPSON. I have some figs.

Enter a MANSERVANT *carrying a dish full of figs.* JEAN *goes on eating them throughout the following scene.*

JEAN: I'm always hungry! It's a kind of bulimia. I hope there are lots of other things to eat in your cupboards.

MADAME SIMPSON. Your father always has something put away.

Enter THE FATHER, *from the back.*

THE FATHER. I've given you an enormous amount of money. You're rich.
JEAN. You gave me five hundred thousand francs; I've only got a hundred thousand left.
LYDIA. There are a whole lot of empty bedrooms here, in this house. We can sometimes sleep in one room, sometimes in another, on the ground floor or on the first floor, or in the attic. You won't be bored, there are some Latin books, some religious books, the whole of theology.
JEAN. They're more or less incomprehensible to me. I used to understand them, before, but I've forgotten, I've parted company with religion.
THE FATHER. Here are some cards.
LYDIA. Tarot cards?

THE FATHER *brings a lot of cards out of his pocket and throws them either on the table or at* JEAN's *feet.*

JEAN *(picking them up).* Tarot cards. What strange pictures! With old words. Even so, I do understand one, here and there.
THE FATHER *(pulling great packets of banknotes out of his pocket and giving them to* JEAN*).* Here! here's some money.
JEAN. They're old Russian banknotes.
THE FATHER. They're Turkish.
JEAN. Russian or Turkish, they're out of date, they're no longer valid. I can't pay Uncle Ernest's debts with this. That's him now, phoning me.

JEAN *goes over to the telephone, which isn't ringing. He puts the receiver to his ear, and then hangs up.*

Yes, that was Uncle Ernest, asking me for a lot of money to pay the family debts.
THE FATHER. I don't want any more to do with that family, they're all vagabonds and failures.
MADAME SIMPSON. That's exactly what I was telling him just now.
JEAN. And anyway, that money, those banknotes—they're the ones Uncle Ernest sent me, to get you to change them into valid notes. I want some other ones!
THE FATHER. It was your mother who sent you here. What a nerve you have! You're just like her! You aren't afraid of me any longer because you know I can't beat you, now.
JEAN. There are some very old people in my mother's family. They're all very old, they aren't like you and me: in spite of everything, we've stayed young. If only you could see how my mother has aged. She's been here for the last eighteen months. If only you could see how she's aged! She looks as old as my grandmother.
MADAME SIMPSON. Then you *have* been to see her! Your father had forbidden you to.
LYDIA. No one can forbid him to go and see his mother.
JEAN. Yes, after a year. She was here, and I didn't go to see her. I had too many obligations, all sorts of business, and worries. And then, there weren't any taxis, there was no bus. I tried to see her several times. There

was always something that made it impossible. Either there was no transport, or I got lost on the way. Or else I met some friends who stopped me and started chatting, and then it got dark and I had to go home.

MADAME SIMPSON. You said you hadn't seen her, and you asked me to try to find her for you.

JEAN. I don't actually know whether I really did see her, whether I really found her. Yes, I did look for her, but I got lost on the way. She lives behind the stadium. (*To* LYDIA). But *you* have seen her; you *have* seen her.

THE FATHER. How could you know that she has aged so much?

JEAN *(still eating figs).* But I tell you I just don't know any more whether I saw *her,* or whether I only saw my grandmother, or whether I saw them both.

THE FATHER. I can't give you any more than four hundred thousand francs. Here's a five-hundred-thousand franc note, give me the change.

JEAN. Here you are.

MADAME SIMPSON. You see—your pockets were full of money.

JEAN. Not enough! I need a whole lot more. The family needs money badly. There are so many of them, and they're all very poor. That's the very least you owe them. And they're all very old.

JEAN *lies down on the divan.*

MADAME SIMPSON. You're well dressed, you look well off.

A fat wallet falls out of JEAN'S *pocket; it is full of banknotes.*

JEAN. I must go and give this money to my mother and her family. But I'll be back; they'll need more than this.

He picks the banknotes up from the ground, and LYDIA *helps him to fill a brief-case with them.*

I'll go and take them all this money. I know where she lives. It's rue Claude-Terrasse. But where is that street?

THE FATHER. We can look it up in the street map!

MADAME SIMPSON. That's not your job. It's none of your business.

THE FATHER. There's a horse-drawn cab in the street, in front of the door. Or rather, it has two horses, and maybe even three.

MADAME SIMPSON (*to* JEAN). You see how indulgent your father is! It isn't my fault if he doesn't give you more money. It wasn't I who took everything. (*To* THE FATHER). Let him fend for himself!

JEAN. A horse-drawn cab, to get to the other side of the town—it won't go fast enough, and it'll cost much too much. Come on, Lydia, we'll go and look for a taxi.

THE FATHER. You know very well there aren't any taxis!

JEAN. Even so, I must hurry.

LYDIA. There may be some trams, or buses, but which is the right one?

JEAN. It's late, it's late, I must hurry!

Enter THE GRANDMOTHER.

LYDIA. Grandmother!

THE FATHER. You've brought the whole family here. Even though I told you not to.
MADAME SIMPSON. It mustn't be forgotten that I am in my own home, here.
THE GRANDMOTHER. It's too late now, your mother's dead!
JEAN (*distressed).* She might have waited a bit longer, she'd already waited so long.
THE FATHER. In the books I gave you, it tells you what to do when you're going to die, or when you've just died.
JEAN. But is all that still true? Because they're old books, very old books, and they're writing about experiences that are very ancient.
MADAME SIMPSON. When I am dying, I want a wreath of flowers put on my head.
LYDIA (*to* JEAN). Calm down.
THE FATHER. I regret her! After all, she was my wife. But what do you want me to do?
JEAN. You might as well give me the book that tells what should be done for someone who's just died.
LYDIA. You can console yourself with your wealth. We own several houses. There are several beds in each house. We can sleep in a different bed every night. You who never like to sleep in the same bed.

Characters. JEAN, LYDIA.

They enter, one from the left, the other from the right, and meet in the middle of the stage.

LYDIA. Have you heard the news, can you believe it, Constantin is becoming more respected and admired every day, he's on the up and up, he's just won the most important literary prize in the world. No one's thinking of giving it to you any more, you're getting further away from it every day! The respect they used to have for you has practically vanished. In some countries, people haven't even heard of you. Even in France, people are forgetting you.
JEAN. That's true; who does still know me? I'm very unlucky. I thought I'd arrived, and there was no more to be done. I didn't realize that I had to go on fighting. I thought I'd carried everything before me, and I threw away my weapons. Whereas the others were going on fighting in obscurity. And then, all of a sudden, the clouds disperse and they appear in the full light of day, the light of celebrity. What can I do to go back and plunge into obscurity again, while I wait for another day?
LYDIA. Constantin has won the world prize. It's out of your reach. You could have had it, though.
JEAN. I fought against my sloth for years. But then I let it overcome me. I sacrified my spiritual life and the salvation of my soul for the sake of my celebrity, and now it's all gone.

LYDIAP. Could you start all over again?
JEAN. I must be very old. How old am I?
LYDIA. There's an official letter for you.

She hands him the letter.

JEAN *(reading it).* 'Dear Sir, Further to your application, you have been awarded a teaching post in a Strasbourg lycée.' I can't be so very old, then! I must even be young, since they're giving me a chance to begin my career again! A school teacher, like when I started out.

Exit LYDIA.

JEAN. Let me see, where am I? Why, I'm in Paris, of course! I've just come from Marseilles, I'd just arrived after a long voyage, I'd been on a cruise, I'd gone to Constantinople. Yes, I was on a huge boat. It was so wide that it had difficulty sailing up the Bosphorus, they'd had to oil it to get it through.

Enter LOUIS.

LOUIS. You wasted you time again, on that voyage, you think you still have time to waste but it's very late, now. You're too old.
JEAN. The psyche has no age! I'm still young. I'm still young in my dreams. The unconscious doesn't age. And I can walk, and I can run.
LOUIS. You had a beautiful dream, a beautiful dream that lasted fifteen years, nearly twenty years, but your beautiful dream is over, you've never done anything for me.
JEAN. You look as if you despise me, you who used to adulate me. That's a splendid suit you're wearing!
LOUIS. It's irreparable! This time it's hopeless! So far you've been lucky enough to get by, but it's all over, now! You're too decrepit—just look at me, see how well I've worn! I shall see you all into your graves! It's my turn to laugh, now. There's no point in your even trying, any more. You've had your day. I'm off. You have to know how to get rid of friendships when they become an encumbrance. I have a date with my beautiful fiancée.

Exit.

JEAN. That Louis! You only have to stop being famous and he drops you, I shall never forgive him! If I have my day again, in spite of everything, I shan't forget this. He's afraid it'll all start up again. He used to envy me so much that he'd gnash his teeth; now he's happy, he's rejoicing at being able to take his revenge. But he won't get it, he won't get it. I shall go to Strasbourg. I have *not* had my day yet, I shall prove it to him. But there's only one train where you don't have to pay. If I miss that train I shall lose everything for good. What can I do not to miss that train, and which station does it go from? I'm afraid of missing that train, of not arriving in time because of this suitcase, it's too heavy to carry, it's chaining me down.

Enter LYDIA.

LYDIA. I can help you carry your suitcase, if you like.

JEAN. Not long ago, only two years ago, I had money coming in from all sides, newspapers used to send me money. Newspapers carrying my photo, but now nothing comes in any more. What can I do to find a bit of money?

LYDIA. In the old days, when we were poor, you used to look on the ground, and you found money on the kerbs, in the gutters. Bend down and look.

JEAN. I'll try.

He bends down and looks.

LYDIA. Look! Over there! There's something glittering! There! and there! . . . .

JEAN *(picking up some coins, and looking at them).* It's nothing at all, little coins that are hardly worth anything. I can't get by with this.

LYDIA. Look!—there too!

JEAN *(bending down again and picking up a coin):* Worthless! These are old coins that have been withdrawn from circulation.

LYDIA. Never mind, there's always that job in Strasbourg waiting for you. I went to the Faculty of Medicine and asked for your diploma. Here it is!

JEAN. An Arts diploma? I shall show it to everyone, so people know I'm still capable of passing exams. But why was it the Faculty of Medicine that gave me this diploma? Do you get Arts degrees there too?

LYDIA. Of course you do, certainly you do—as you see! It even carries more weight than a Faculty of Arts, it's more scientific. The great scientists and medical men appreciate you. That's because they knew you at the clinic where you had your operation. Don't you remember how they cosseted you? Go to the station and give the clerk this diploma; they'll give you a ticket in exchange for it.

JEAN: I must go away. It's sinister, living here.

LYDIA. The country starts quite close to Paris, at the porte de Versailles. You could go there every day.

JEAN. Yes, that's true. I used to, in the old days, I used to go there from time to time, to get some fresh air and to revel in the beauty of the countryside. I used to go there, too, when they let me out of the clinic between two operations; there are some big fields, and a little hill. They give you new heart. Yes, I can see it now, that little hill, and I can see that bit of the country, it was so luminous. That light! It was a light that was different from light. And then, we used to climb up the hill, and right at the top, at the summit, we came to the luminous city. I went there several times. Was it in a dream or in reality? In reality! But it was so beautiful that I thought I was dreaming. What's the name of that city, with its white houses and its sky? There were white houses bathed in sunlight, and such a beautiful square, all lit up. What's the name of that town?

LYDIA. Aluminia. Aluminia was what it was called.

JEAN. You see, I haven't lost everything, because I can remember the name of the town. Aluminia, Aluminia. I can find it on the map. It's shown on every dream map. Aluminia, town of my heart, Aluminia, town of my dreams, Aluminia, town of my true reality.

LYDIA. We only have to say the name of Aluminia, and all its sun reaches us here.

JEAN. Then why do the shadows keep coming back? Light—stay! Aluminia, name of light! Oh, but everything is clouding over. I haven't enough strength left to keep Aluminia's luminosity in me. It's got dark again. Have I stopped dreaming? Or is it a nightmare? Once again, my heart is possessed by darkness.
LYDIA. You'll find the light again in Strasbourg.

Enter PAUL. *Exit* LYDIA.

JEAN. You've arrived with the dark. Only a moment ago I was in Aluminia. But now, Aluminia has retreated a long, long way away. You're still well dressed. In comparison with me, you seem even better dressed. You mustn't be angry with me if I tell you straightaway that I need money for my train ticket. I can't walk there. I used to walk up the hill, and Aluminia was immediately revealed. But now I'm too tired to walk uphill, or even to walk on the flat. I need money to buy my train ticket.

After a pause:

People appear, they yell, they exhaust themselves, they walk, they talk, they whisper, they fight one another, they insult one another, they make it up, they re-insult each other, they are envious, they are jealous, they steal from each other, they torture each other, and then they fade away, they disappear. Some go and stay in splendid country inns. Others come to the door of the inn and shout, they go in and chase the others out. Often, there's fire and smoke, everything goes up in flames. They rebuild. Then it's the turn of others to occupy the best places, they're there for two days, after four days they're still there. Then they too are chased out, dragged out, they have to uproot themselves, and then they too disappear.

'We're just passing by . . .', they say, but in fact they entrench themselves. The badly-lodged ones also dig themselves in. No one wants to disappear amicably, in friendly fashion. The most affluent are just as ruthless as the most impoverished, but it's the poor who get the most satisfaction—from their very poverty. There are so many earthquakes, I tell them, so many volcanoes disgorging their flames and their scalding lava on to us. There are so many fires in the forests and towns. So many storms and cyclones. And then there are so many lethal epidemics. Let them do their worst.

Since in any case we're going to burn, let's not burn with impatience. Let's dance in a ring, instead, or else, even though there are such infinite numbers of us, let's go hand in hand, or arm in arm, towards the eternity of nothingness, the heavens of silence. Rather than entrench ourselves, let's speed it up, come on, let's make a dash for it.

Alas, who can guarantee that we're only in the outer circle. The next one may well be worse.

TWO WOMEN *appear.*

Tell me which way I should go.
FIRST WOMAN. The cardinal points aren't the same.
SECOND WOMAN. There are super-Souths and super-Norths.
FIRST WOMAN. A river like a magic carpet.
SECOND WOMAN. You must go back to the periphery.

Characters: VIOLETTE, JEAN.

VIOLETTE *is wearing a dressing gown, under which she is naked.*

JEAN. You're Violette, I recognize you. You're just as young and beautiful as you used to be. It's amazing, you haven't changed a bit in the last twenty-five years, you're still twenty-five. I'm amazed at how young you are. What an irreparable pity! What a pity that Alexandre is dead! Don't look at me so unkindly. I know; you must be angry with me. Are you still angry with me?

VIOLETTE. Yes, I'm still angry with you. Though perhaps not for the reasons you think, you were young and ambitious, you were stupid with him. But it isn't only that . . . it's not that.

JEAN. I was young and ambitious, but so were all three of us. Our friendship lasted such a short time! Oh, you don't know how I regret his death!

VIOLETTE. What's the use of remorse? I will concede, though, that you do feel it.

JEAN. Before he died, he made a gesture—he sent me his photo.

VIOLETTE. You sent him yours at the same time.

JEAN. We both had the same idea, without realizing it.

VIOLETTE: Your photos crossed in the post. He died four days later.

JEAN: How did I hear of it? He was so ill, and he'd become so weak, he couldn't stand the strain.

VIOLETTE. People said I'd abandoned him. They said it was after a quarrel. That was slander.

JEAN. That last gesture—it was a sort of farewell. Do you believe we shall never see him again? Is there another world?

VIOLETTE. There is no other world. If we let an opportunity slip here, it's gone for ever. Nothing is retrievable.

JEAN. Then you really think there is no other world?

VIOLETTE: There are no other spaces, there are no other places, there are no other times.

JEAN. There may be other sorts of interlinked spaces, separated by imaginary curtains, or by partitions. There may be times in the same time, at the same time joined and separated.

VIOLETTE. Don't be childish, and don't ask the foolish questions everyone else asks. Everything only happens once.

JEAN. Alexandre wasn't so sure. I often surprised him kissing icons . . . No no, don't look like that, it wasn't simply fetishism.

Pause.

I lived passionately, in those days. It was an intense, prolific, fruitful time. Things happened. But for years now time has become empty, distorted . . . time flies. Its moments pass me by. The river used to flow slowly, but today it's become a cataract. Its moments used to caress me, to linger . . . I have arrived. But where? I have succeeded—in what? Everything is hollow. What we should die of, is love.

VIOLETTE. You obviously disagreed a lot, there was a misunderstanding. Everything is a misunderstanding.

JEAN. That's what he used to say.
VIOLETTE. I have a new man friend. He's explained it all to me—the reasons for that misunderstanding. You didn't behave well.
JEAN. Who is your friend?
VIOLETTE. Didn't you know? He's Jan, the Pole.
JEAN. You don't know Polish.
VIOLETTE. I translate from the English.
JEAN. It's written in French.
VIOLETTE. The English version is better.
JEAN. You can't imagine, Violette, how much I regret letting such a long, long time go by without seeing Alexandre! Though remorse is futile, of course. I was so stupid—perhaps we both were! He was my best friend, my brother. How was it that we became estranged?
VIOLETTE: You avoided him!
JEAN. I thought he was copying me. And in fact, he did steal a dream from me.
VIOLETTE. He used to dream a lot, too. It's true that you could have been brothers. You were both so proud of being literary men. You were so alike, you used to have the same dreams. You had the same sort of past. And also, the same fears, the same obsessions.
JEAN. It was all nonsense; an imaginary literary rivalry.
VIOLETTE. Your fault. You were afraid! In actual fact, it was only you who got anything out of your friendship.
JEAN. But he had become a militant. Though what difference did that make? It was stupid of me.
VIOLETTE. You ought to have realized that earlier! I can't be friends with you any more.
JEAN. Don't hate me so much! I've always been incapable of being friends with anyone who didn't share my ideas.
VIOLETTE. Did you really have any ideas? Ideas! If he became a militant, it was probably because of your split-up; he wouldn't have, if you hadn't deserted him. If he joined the Party, it was to have a family. You'd left him completely helpless. Ideas! Ideologies! They have more to do with luck than with choice. Accidents. Antics. Absurdities.
JEAN. Yet I always maintain that friendship ought to be above all that sort of thing. Friendship, no matter what. Friendship is so wonderful; that, and death, are the only things of any importance. In the end, he chose death.
VIOLETTE. He was chosen by death.
JEAN. Twenty years have gone by: twenty years! How can I have managed to live without him? Never again, never again!
VIOLETTE. You bore me, with your guilt. Go on, then, wallow in the mud of your guilt! Wallow in it! I can't do anything about it.
JEAN. But it was you, Violette, who made things worse. I tried, several times, to see you both again, to make it up. You rebuffed me, you cold-shouldered me. I realized that you didn't want to forget. You made things worse.
VIOLETTE. Perhaps you should have persevered! But all that's behind me, now; I have a new friend, and I have to translate his work.

JEAN. But perhaps . . . perhaps it was you who were tired of him, you couldn't stand it any longer. He needed too much support, he needed help at every instant of his life, from morning to night, from night to morning. The moment he woke up you used to put his cigarette in his mouth. After that, it was his baby's bottle filled with spirits. He had to have that before he'd get up. There was certainly a misunderstanding at the start, but you took advantage of it, you dug this misunderstanding deeper, instead of filling it in. You were lucid, you knew what you were doing. You could have helped him, you could have helped us, you could have explained things. You didn't want to smooth things over. Why not? What was the real reason? There must be a reason I can't fathom, a reason you hid from me. What was the real reason?
VIOLETTE. Have you really forgotten?

She lets her dressing gown drop to the ground, and remains naked in front of JEAN.

ALEXANDRE *appears at the back.*

ALEXANDRE. Go on, Jean, you have my permission. Go on, since you have my permission! Don't you think she's beautiful, don't you love her? Can't you love her? You'd be doing me a favour!
VIOLETTE (*to* ALEXANDRE). Is he an idiot, or is he just pretending?
ALEXANDRE. Jean, you disappoint me, you really disappoint me.
JEAN. You're beautiful, you're radiant! I couldn't believe my eyes, I didn't dare, I was rooted to the spot. You shouldn't have been offended, I didn't dare believe it. How could I have imagined . . . ?
VIOLETTE. Never a second chance!

Pause

ALEXANDRE. I preferred to die. I wanted to write works that were as beautiful as music, as sweet, as tender, as pathetic, as serene. Even poetry can't do that. Sometimes, but it's rare, there's a ballet of words, there's verbal music: with Aragon, for instance, but it's so very rare. Even in Aragon.

ALEXANDRE *disappears.* JEAN *remains, as if rooted to the spot, facing* VIOLETTE, *who slowly puts her dressing gown on again.*

VIOLETTE. No, never a second chance.

Characters: JEAN, ALEXANDRE.

JEAN. Nothing new exists. Every so often we have the impression that we've discovered a wood worth exploring, a little copse. We believe it to be a new continent—but at the far end of the copse, and even in the copse itself, we find the traces of our own footsteps. We've been there before! We're amazed . . . and then we remember exactly when it was, the precise day, the precise hour. Disappointing!

ALEXANDRE. There might well be another adventure!

JEAN. Then we'd have to break through the barriers, leap over the wall... I can't bring myself to do that.

ALEXANDRE. It isn't easy! In reality, we adore retracing our steps. The same white wine every morning, the first cigarette. A new day is dawning. We even like the habits we've got into, however uncomfortable they may be.

JEAN. We *would* like to start all over again, though—on condition that everything was new. But we want the newness to be just what we expect. We like starting again, but we don't like starting. And yet, and yet . . .

ALEXANDRE. The little marionettes do three pirouettes, and then they disappear.

JEAN. Or else they don't want to disappear. That would be all right, perhaps, if other people didn't want us to disappear. *We* have no wish to disappear. They look at us, they listen to us; and we look at ourselves and listen to ourselves. And they say: They're the same marionettes.

ALEXANDRE. We say the same thing about ourselves. We know we're past it.

JEAN. If only we and the others could rediscover the freshness of that first morning!

ALEXANDRE. A little white wine would help us! No no!—just to get tipsy, not drunk!

JEAN. I'm a bourgeois at heart, which means that I cling to my habits.

ALEXANDRE. To do something different!

JEAN. To be something different! A totally unexpected being, an inconceivable, yes yes, an unimaginable being!

ALEXANDRE. A change of scenery!

JEAN. Oh yes, a change of scenery, a new country! I'm tempted by the thought of a new country. But I'm also very much afraid of it.

ALEXANDRE. I'm fed up with this country. And I don't want a different one.

JEAN. If we could only have some idea, just a little idea, of the new country, if we knew it, then we wouldn't feel out of place. I don't know whether I like adventure or whether I have a horror of it. I sometimes tell myself that I never want to have another adventure.

ALEXANDRE. Boredom and fatigue end by giving you a taste for adventure.

JEAN. Boredom! I've got used to that. You get used to it, or rather, you don't get used to it, but you get used to not getting used to it.

ALEXANDRE. And yet things aren't all that wonderful. Why don't we start again, and do better?

JEAN. The conditions wouldn't be anything like the same! Even the word 'condition' might lose its meaning.

ALEXANDRE. We shall always be conditioned by other conditions. What it comes down to, perhaps, is that we can change our skin, but we can't change our being. What we call our skin, that is, though we don't know what is might be called in the future.

JEAN. Will existence always exist? Will we be able to call it "existence"? What sort of existence? We might "do better"! Unless we're a total failure, a metaphysical failure, once and for all, once and for all our existences, our quasi-existences.

ALEXANDRE. Do better the next time round! Is that possible?

JEAN. That would be quite good enough. Though we don't even have the gift of ubiquity.

ALEXANDRE. And yet it isn't much to ask. I too have the impression that I'm living in a cage. I'm even positive that we're in a cage. It has a door, which we should be able to find. Which I *shall* find, one day. But whatever happens, it must be found. We're being crowded out by other people. They arrive in their hordes, and fill the whole cage. Ah, if we only had another, less congested cage!

JEAN. It would still be a cage.

ALEXANDRE: Were we put on this earth to live in a cage for ever?

JEAN. That's just what I was saying. What's the use of changing cages? But the decision doesn't rest with us! We might just as well live in the same cage.

ALEXANDRE. You couldn't. If you're already bored, that's because you'd rather go somewhere else. You've already accepted the idea of adventure. And the others are crowding us out.

JEAN. A little corner would be enough for me!

ALEXANDRE. There won't be any quiet little corners much longer! They've gone for good. You can see, you can see them, they're besieging you, they're devouring you.

JEAN. What you say both worries and reassures me: that boredom by its very nature makes us like adventure, makes us long for adventure. No, though; that's not so sure. I shall stay here a little longer, as long as I can. With the two or three people I love. I don't want to leave them on their own.

ALEXANDRE. Personally, I think I shall be able to cut loose. I don't want to be shown the door, I shall plunge into adventure.

JEAN. The endless abyss of adventure! To leap over the wall! But what if it's into an abyss?

ALEXANDRE. Man has already taken his first steps on the moon. Those men had enough courage! You only need just a little bit more courage! I'm not going to wait until I'm shown the door.

JEAN. Strange. Such a tiny little village, and they've built three enormous skyscrapers. The few people who live there are in the country, yet at the same time they have the comforts of big towns. Do they have a lift to take them up to the top? And the other houses are very small, but there are two streets, two cinemas, and two restaurants, rustic restaurants.

THE YOUNG VILLAGER. What are you doing here?

JEAN. I'm looking for the space there used to be. *(Aside):* He looks like a lummox.

THE YOUNG VILLAGER. If you're looking for the little castle, you have to go through the little wood. A Count used to live there, in days gone by. They've turned it into a hospital, now.

JEAN. You look like Victor McLaglen—you know, the film star. You look like a thug.

THE YOUNG VILLAGER. I'm thirty years old. I failed the exams to get into the first form at school, I don't know whether I shall sit them again or go to a Technical College. I'd like to punch you in the ribs.

JEAN. Wouldn't you rather come and have a drink with me?

THE YOUNG VILLAGER: Ah, here's my father.

Enter another, older, VILLAGER, *who is extraordinarily like the young one.*

JEAN. You're so alike! Your father could be your older brother. You both have a black patch over your left eye.

THE SECOND VILLAGER. My bar is over there, it's very close. Come and have a drink with me.

JEAN. I've got a lot of money on me. Look.

He shows him some banknotes.

THE YOUNG VILLAGER. Who gave you those?

JEAN. The baker. He changed my letter of credit for me.

THE SECOND VILLAGER. They aren't worth anything. He's cheated you. They're promissory notes.

JEAN. Promissory notes?

THE SECOND VILLAGER. They haven't been valid since the last war.

JEAN. This is where I lived when I was a boy. Don't you remember me? I used to live in the Mill. The farm that was called the Mill.

THE YOUNG VILLAGER: Not at all. What about you, Dad? Where was the farm?

JEAN: By that little stream. Behind the copse. Don't you really know? Haven't you ever heard of its former owners? They were called Miller—and their family had lived in this region for ages. It's a pity the house has been demolished, there's nothing left of it. Not even the memory of it. And yet that was what I came to look for. I shan't come back to this village. But where shall I spend my holidays?

Set: dark, dismal room. Enter, right, JEAN *and a* FRIEND. *The ceiling is dark and dirty. The sound of an old woman moaning and groaning can be heard coming from the ceiling.*

JEAN. Oh yes, my dear fellow, I have a very beautiful house in the country, half-way between the sea and the mountains, a very different house from the one I really live in. It's a palace, with big salons, Louis Seize furniture, and Empire settees. Louis Treize must certainly have lived there, but it's a house I see in my dreams. As I see it very often in my dreams, it must be a real house. It's a palace, as I told you, and it contains castles that are even bigger than palaces, the grounds of the castles extend as far as the ocean and even farther. How can castles bigger than palaces be contained in palaces? That's a mystery that has something to do with the spaces between-two-worlds, or the spaces between-three-worlds. . . These are spaces that interlock or overlap, this is something you can only understand in a dream, and since I tell you that I often see this house in my dreams, it corresponds to a real house, a totally real house.

THE FRIEND. If Louis Treize lived there, it certainly must be a real house.

JEAN. We've often met there; I meet you in my dreams much more often than I do in this false reality. It's there that we talk about the single and the multiple.

THE FRIEND. I remember it very well, I remember it perfectly. I'm an industrialist, we often used to talk there about my sock factory, as well, about the multiplication of socks. How can a sock become multiple? I discovered new materials, neither silk, nor nylon, nor cotton, nor the other materials and fabrics that are so common in everyday reality. And yet this isn't the first time we've met in this dark house in the rue Claude-Terrasse, which must also be your house, and just as real as the other one, as we're here so often, in this dark ground floor, in this so very dark ground floor where we've eaten bread, where we've also drunk a lot of beer, and had a lot of philosophical discussions. Whereabouts do you place this house, in your dream-spaces? Is there a distance between the spaces, and then other spaces in space? There must be, otherwise we couldn't be here.

JEAN. Real houses are the ones we remember, but also, and above all, they're the houses we remember in our dreams, the houses we rediscover and enter in our dreams.

The sound of an old woman moaning and groaning can be heard coming from the ceiling.

The real house is the one we dream of, yes, I dream just as often of the one we're in now, they're all real, but which is the most real of all the real ones? I never dream of a third house, it doesn't exist, and it's this one we're in that I dream of the most often, so this one is the most real.

THE FRIEND. Of course this one is the most real, because it's the house you lived in with your mother.

JEAN. Yes, that's precisely it, you're right, this one is the most real, it's the most real because it's the house I lived in with my mother. She thought I was mad, I've come to look for her.

Moans and groans from the ceiling.

She's the one who's mad, one shouldn't say that about one's mother, but she's hiding. Look, the house is empty, there's only just one little table, to stop people looking for her behind the chairs, but I don't know why this house resembles her, it still contains her invisible gestures, her sad face, and the floor is covered with her tears, which never dry.

THE FRIEND. They won't stop flowing until you find her, can't you hear that weeping and wailing coming from the ceiling and falling, drop by drop? Look—there's one on the palm of my hand.

JEAN. She's upstairs. Mother, you're there, you're upstairs. Come down.

THE OLD WOMAN'S VOICE. I'm afraid, downstairs, the floor's worm-eaten. Cockroaches have been born from my tears, there's a lot of vermin on the floor, the floor's worm-eaten, the grave is under the floor, I don't want to fall into it, all my relations are in it, turned to dust. Up there I was preserved from death and dust.

JEAN *(looking up).* But I swear I've been looking for you everywhere. I've found you at last, Mother.

THE OLD WOMAN'S VOICE. I don't want to come down.

JEAN *and* THE FRIEND *raise their arms and pull on the feet of the armchair that can be seen from below. The whole of the armchair appears, with* THE OLD WOMAN *sitting in it.* JEAN *and* THE FRIEND *take hold of it and gently put it down on the ground.*

JEAN. You see, the floor hasn't cracked, Mama.

THE FRIEND. You see, Madame, the floor hasn't collapsed, the vermin are running away from you.

THE OLD WOMAN *(in her armchair).* I don't want to, I didn't want to, I'm afraid, you left me alone too long, I'm not used to solitude. (*To* JEAN): Where's your sister? Where's your father? (*Pointing to* THE FRIEND): Who is that man? But you aren't going to leave me here, are you!

JEAN. I'm going to take you away, I shall put you in the most beautiful glass sarcophagus, like the ones the Italian popes have, you shall have a red dress.

THE OLD WOMAN. You can see how disgusting I am, my dresses are all torn. I've got nothing but rags left, I'm nothing but bone and a very little skin, a thin layer of skin.

JEAN. Everyone will come and see you.

THE OLD WOMAN *(pointing to* THE FRIEND*)*: I asked you who that man was.

JEAN. Don't you recognize him? why, he's Georges, my school friend who used to come to tea with us, the one I used to play truant with.

THE OLD WOMAN (*showing* JEAN *her claws*). You didn't answer when I asked you why you left me alone so long.

JEAN. I've been looking for you everywhere.

THE OLD WOMAN. You didn't really want to find me, you were in your palaces and castles with your lady friends, you didn't think about me, you were living in your father's house, he was much richer.

THE FRIEND. He's been dead a long time, too.

THE OLD WOMAN. But with all his money, he could afford to give some to the church, and his house is appropriate to the dead, he has furniture and food. Life isn't fair, and death isn't fair, either. And what about you? Yes yes yes, you were pretending to be looking for me.

JEAN. I've looked for you in all the cemeteries, in old people's homes, at your sister's and your cousin's, among the living and the dead, I looked for you in parish registers, but I didn't find your name, Mama.

THE OLD WOMAN. That's because you never had any Masses said for me. When you were looking for me in this house, you never looked upstairs, you only looked at the worm-eaten floor, then you made your escape as fast as you could, you were afraid, you were ashamed, and yet I really am your mother and I shall recognize you until the end of the world, until after the end of the world, and I shall find you in limbo, even higher up than that, in the Pleiades. Where am I now? In the common grave, the paupers' grave, but I was on the look-out and I hid above the ceiling, and that's why this house hasn't fallen into ruin, in spite of its decrepitude. And I shall make its foundations tremble, and I shall sow chaos in it.

THE FRIEND (*to* JEAN). She isn't your mother. Your mother was gentle. This is your grandmother.

THE OLD WOMAN. Both his grandmother and his grandfather.

THE FATHER *(entering, to* THE GRANDMOTHER*).* No doubt you're imagining doubtful things.

THE OLD WOMAN (THE GRANDMOTHER). It is doubtful that I am imagining doubtful things.

THE FATHER. Just because you imagine things that are certain, that doesn't mean they aren't doubtful.

THE OLD WOMAN (*to* THE FATHER). So you're here?

THE FATHER (*to* THE OLD WOMAN). Do you believe you're more alive now, because you're dead? No, you don't exist any more now than you did before, when you did exist. I haven't wronged you—no more than anyone can wrong a person who believes he is still alive.

THE OLD WOMAN. Yes you have. Look, I'm more alive than before, because during my lifetime I didn't have these nails I have now, they weren't so long, so sharp. Move this chair for me, to make it into a judge's bench, and put that table in front of it, like a table in court, with a black cloth. Do you understand?

She says this to THE FRIEND.

You see, here they all come, one after the other. I am the Seat of Judgment, I am the representative of the judges. God is just, but He is also All-terrible. You didn't know that God is a man who doesn't always pardon.

THE FRIEND *seats her at the table, and turns the armchair into a kind of throne.*

THE FATHER (*to* THE OLD WOMAN). Everything we have done on earth is of no value, of no importance. The worst crimes and the best deeds belong to the world of the living, but all that is null, and void, both for the other world and for the people in the other world.

THE OLD WOMAN. If you think *you* aren't alive, either, why, in the world of the non-living, are you afraid of what you too call my claws, my talons my S-hooks?

And you, my son, come and stand on my right hand, and be my assessor. Bring in the guilty.

Enter the Father's second wife (MADAME SIMPSON, *that is.) She is old, outrageously dressed, and made up to look much younger, like a whore.*

So here you are, you witch. You drove my daughter out of the house, I'm going to get you by the throat with my claws, they're stronger than living claws, stronger and more painful for the non-living, who haven't one more drop of blood to lose, because blood cures, but you haven't any blood left. I'm not afraid of pistols, or daggers, or knives.

Enter a CAPTAIN, *one of Madame Simpson's two brothers, and her other brother,* THE TOP CIVIL SERVANT.

And here you are, too, my son's second brother-in-law, you who had all my family shot, you're the person I've been waiting for for such a very, very long time. You, you ridiculous captain, with your epaulettes, your medals and your sabre. What's the use of all that finery here, why did you kill, shoot all my family? I knew you wouldn't escape me, I am Justice. No, I'm more than that—I am Vengeance.

THE CAPTAIN. Because they didn't belong to my caste. I presided over our national army's courts martial, I had orders to kill people who didn't belong to my caste. I was respected, saluted, decorated. I was proud of what I did, yes, I had to exterminate everyone who didn't belong to my caste, so that my caste should live. I also killed, I also condemned all the lukewarm members of my caste, all the cowards who thought they were brave. I was cheered in the streets, my summings-up were the best, the most powerful, the most persuasive.

THE FRIEND (*to* THE OLD WOMAN). The people of his race were killed, too, to the last man, by another race. He is the only survivor out of all the dead of his race, the race that killed his race has also been exterminated by another race. No one knows the names of all these races any more, of all the dozens of races that have exterminated each other.

THE OLD WOMAN (*to* THE FRIEND). You're a bad advocate. (*to* THE CAPTAIN). And who were the advocates? Who defended the thousands of condemnable people who were condemned?

THE CAPTAIN. They didn't need advocates. They pleaded guilty. Or else they were already dead when they were sentenced.

THE OLD WOMAN. You'll pay too, you too will pay for all the ethnic groups that massacred your ethnic groups whose names have been forgotten. The Demiurge himself has forgotten the names of those billions of combatants or murderers, you're doubly dead, I condemn you and I shall also condemn your brother, the great civil servant, who used to steal the land from the poor, though they didn't deserve to have any, either. But I shall decide who are ultra-guilty—more guilty than the guilty. I can see no innocence, and the Demiurge is having a good laugh at this Judgment, and I'm pronouncing this Judgment so that he can have an even better laugh. Clowns that we are. I condemn you.

THE CAPTAIN. Don't do that. Let the dead survive in death, as well as the fifty dead men who are still dying in the fire. I don't want to be reduced to dust.

THE FRIEND (*to* THE OLD WOMAN). There are still other races, the very last ones, who are massacring each other under the eye of the Demiurge.

THE OLD WOMAN. Let them come back, they can all appear before me, and I'll massacre them.

THE FRIEND *pushes* THE CAPTAIN *into* THE OLD WOMAN'S *claws.*

THE OLD WOMAN (*squeezing* THE CAPTAIN'S *throat*). Smile, handsome Captain, smile.

She plunges her other hand into his skull.

Your brains are all red and black, I'm going to smear them over your eyes, and stuff them up your nose and in your mouth. Smile, then, Captain, and scream if you can, I'm going to shove my hand down your throat. Do you remember, handsome Captain, how you used to swagger in your beautiful, well-polished boots, and what a swashbuckler you were with your sabre? I'll give you two seconds to speak.

THE CAPTAIN. I was only obeying orders, with my summings-up. I had pity.

THE OLD WOMAN. It's because you had pity that I'm taking your sabre, which you wanted to stick in the belly of my daughter, my son-in-law's wife. I'm going to stick it into your own belly, into the ghosts of your guts, and now I'm going to tear out your monocled right eye. (The Captain's eye hangs out.) For a second, I'll leave your other eye open, so you can see what's happening to you. You others—watch!

She tears off THE CAPTAIN'S *epaulettes, gold braid and short overcoat.*

You don't need a General or a Colonel to strip you of your rank.

THE CAPTAIN. The law, oh, the law!

THE CAPTAIN *screams, and then falls silent. He collapses.*

THE OLD WOMAN. Don't take his boots off. He only has a living man's feet, and they stink.

THE CAPTAIN *remains spreadeagled on the ground.*

And you, you witch, come over here, no matter how frightened you are, you still have your curls and your beautiful low-cut dress, you might almost be young, but come on, come closer. (MADAME SIMPSON *goes closer.*) As young and beautiful as ever. That's what you think. I'm going to deal with you myself.

She leaves her chair and walks with a limp.

You wanted to inherit everything from my son, my son's whole fortune, and you had magicians to make you more beautiful every day. You hold yourself straight . . . you'll see . . .

And all the rest of you: Watch!

She snatches off her hat, which goes rolling over on the floor, and hits her hard over the shoulders with her stick, which gives MADAME SIMPSON *a stoop. She tears her dress and underwear, takes off her shoes, and, with her clawlike nails, pulls off her false nose and scratches off her make-up.*

MADAME SIMPSON *now has a permanent stoop, and seems older than* THE GRANDMOTHER. THE GRANDMOTHER *has turned an apparently young woman into a naked, hunchbacked old woman.*

THE GRANDMOTHER *starts laughing.*

Look at her, all of you, see how, without her jewels and finery, this is the woman she really is.

She kicks her. MADAME SIMPSON *falls to the ground.*

Get up.
MADAME SIMPSON. I can't get up.

THE GRANDMOTHER *takes her by the scruff of the neck and picks her up.*

I'm cold, I'm frightened, I'm sorry. I oughtn't to have done it.
THE OLD WOMAN. Stupid whore, walk. You're going to walk.

She puts the two sticks into her hands. THE GRANDMOTHER *now moves with agility, and* MADAME SIMPSON *walks, weeping, limping, with the aid of the two sticks.*

THE FRIEND. That's enough, Madame.
JEAN. That's enough; pardon her.
THE OLD WOMAN (*still walking with the same agility, to* MADAME SIMPSON). I've taken your false youth. Who ever pardoned anyone in the world below, or in the world above? You've lost all your powers, you witch, and you've given me back mine. And what about you, mister top civil servant?
THE TOP CIVIL SERVANT. I distributed land to all the peasants who didn't have any. If I was sometimes unfair, it was by mistake. We don't always get our sums right, that's the fault of mathematics.
THE OLD WOMAN. Liar!

She slaps his face.

THE TOP CIVIL SERVANT. You are insulting one of the most senior civil servants in the State.
THE OLD WOMAN. Imbecile. *(She gives him two more slaps.)* Where are the peasants you spared, where are they? Let them come and bear witness.
THE TOP CIVIL SERVANT. They are no longer of the earth.
THE OLD WOMAN. Then let the earth bear witness.

THE TOP CIVIL SERVANT *brings a small bag out of his pocket and drops a little of the earth it contains.*

That earth won't speak. It won't speak, because it is no longer earth. Just look down at your feet; that earth isn't there. There is no more earth, there is no more sky; there is no more world.

THE TOP CIVIL SERVANT. I have no more tomb, where is my tomb, r monument? No one will know who I was. I am . . . I am . . . my name is . . . I was who? Who was I?

He collapses.

THE OLD WOMAN. You are everything, and at the same time you are nothing, in the empty spaces which are not spaces.

Enter a beautiful GYPSY GIRL.

My daughter was humiliated by her husband, but you humiliated his second wife, and I have nothing against you. I shan't awaken my daughter. The only pardon that can be given is to let the dead rest in peace. Hang your lover, hang him by the neck, since you say you loved him. Take this rope.

THE GYPSY GIRL *goes over to* THE FATHER.

Drag him behind you.

THE GYPSY GIRL *does so.*

And let all this lot disappear for centuries, for centuries and centuries. I shall call you back, and you'll meet me again.

THE OLD WOMAN *takes off her rags and her big false nose: she is young and beautiful, she sings, or rather, she utters loud cries of joy, which are completely inhuman.*

THE CAPTAIN, THE TOP CIVIL SERVANT, *and* MADAME SIMPSON *stand up; they support* THE FATHER *between them, and all go out, laughing.*

A mist rises over the whole stage. It lasts for a few seconds and then the stage reappears, empty.

While the mist lasts, laughs and sounds resembling sobs can be heard. Then they disappear, at the same time as the mist.

Set: Bare. Bright light. In an armchair in the centre, a middle-aged character. Vague rustling sounds and murmurs can be heard coming from the wings.

THE NARRATOR (*or* JEAN), *(without moving from his chair, and only rarely making a gesture with his hand).* I don't know. I don't know. It seemed to me that the horizon was obstructing the green clouds. The avenues were walking about in invalids' pyjamas. Millions of exploding beings, beings—at least they thought they were beings. The façades of the processions were blowing against the monstrous sources of the winds.

THE CHARACTER, *or* JEAN, *speaks in a very clear voice, makes frequent pauses, and respects the punctuation marks. He looks as if he is remembering, or seeing, or dreaming, keeping his eyes wide open.*

Triangles, circles, other surfaces, other volumes, creak, or quiver, waiting for other Pythagorases. I'm amazed that it isn't dark. Are we in intermastery, here? Stone clocks whose mechanisms have taken our appetites away? We are in magazine factories, the warehouse doors are permanently closed. We no longer come from the Pyrenees. They don't look as if they're going to give us the keys. Enigmas neither die nor live. I wasn't expecting this. Yes, though—I *was* expecting it. I left the somnambulistic world because I didn't want to be plunged into another one. There are old men's beards all along the highways, all down the alleyways, and marchionesses collar them. How can they do that, when marchionesses wear neither open collars nor butterfly collars?

Pause.

No, though; that has nothing to do with what I'm seeing. I've lost my command of language. The more I say, the less I speak. The more I speak, the less I say. What do the old-time reasoners do, who reason without reason? I must keep quiet, I have no reason to criticize, and I mustn't. Have I still got my lips? The lips of my dreams? Did I say impatience? Forgive my impatience.

Is impatience a long patience? Like the genius of George Strasser. I've got the wrong lock. Two thousand five hundred books of two thousand five hundred pages, that's too much, even for a life that lasts eight hundred and eighty-eight years. I had French publishers, Michel, Claudius, Gaston. What did they call Pichard, Clovis, and Gerdrard? Gerdrard, the King of the Franks; Clovis, the King of the Cunts. My companions have disappeared. My companions were accompanying me. That sentence makes sense. Does a sensible voice have a choice between blood and sense? They used to have names. Not the same ones. Names get changed in the crucible. I was standing at a street corner, talking to my main publisher and the President of the Republic. No. It was the Republic of the President. No. It was the President of the Republic. What was a republic like, what was a president like? Come on, children, he was saying, let's get back to England in d'Artagnan's boat. D'Artagnan wrote Dupain's books, and Duparc's, and those of the two Dumas, Dumas père and Dumas fils. Dumas father and son: which was the father of the one, and which was the son of the father? Which means: What does it matter? They told me it would all come back to me. Will my caterpillar come back? The porridge was tougher than the meat. What was it they told me? That animals are men who can speak. Does he know what he's talking about? Seeing that I myself can disentangle it. But there isn't any 'seeing that' in this region. Not less, not more, and not yet. It's more difficult to get at than the inner tube of a tyre. There are still something like reminiscences. I beg my own pardon. Comparisons don't exist.

Pause.

There are still—the word 'still' doesn't exist. There are reminiscences, scences, sciences, patiences, rallences, abstinences, parences, recompenses. My afflence, called virulence, had a red breast. Oh dear dear!

Pause.

Is there a bridge? The knights-errant of insolence haven't tasted the hillows of the shoulders. Let's see. Is that permissible? An effort. Let's think, let's think, in spite of the forbiddance. I must be in the world of the resulites. I've come into the festalite of the rebuttites. Let's see: in between, there might be the festival of carnal. No, that's not it. Are the parrots in the pit going to play in the wing? In the wing! ha ha ha! There *was* a wing. Let's see: do the 'let's sees' see the 'let's sees'? The menders of see-saw doors. Here again we're hugging the walls of the inquietudes of inexactitudes. Ah: at last a peach of a phrase. A luminous beach, a thucid prace.

Pause.

Thucid.

Pause.

Thucid. I'd love to be able to speak, and say that thucid and thucidades are the same word. A truel word. Are the same word, are the same bird. Ah, the solitudes of the proscenium. Have I been speaking words?

Terrified:

Have I been speaking words? Ah, the solitudes of the sceniprosium. Have I been speaking, have I been speaking, matonobri. The knights-errant of insolence haven't tasted the hillows of the shoulders, or the head on my grandmother's pillows.

This has nothing to do with what I'm doing, or what I'm seeing. Oh dear dear, is there a bridge? The river, with its running water, has been banished from it. Was the water running, or was it the current that was running the water? The bridge was running; when you were on the river, you crossed it.

Pause.

Were there any? Were there any bridges? You used to hold out your hands to one another from one bridge to the next, but they held you down by your feet.

Pause.

It seems you shouldn't say that, convey that, read that, concede that, remember that, dismember that, curse that, worse that. Memory is forbidden. Bala, bala, balabala, carrionumbala.

My poor head. Ah yes, that was a word. What have I got in its place? Croakeys, sawksquays. The charm and refinement of a chest of drawers is due to the cabinet maker. The cabinet maker on duty is drawn by the chest. They've made false relations out of the present historic. Nice work! What's the point of this irony?

Pause.

In one of those towns which is as charming as France, and evocative of our manomaniac century, they were no white inferior to the white tiles created by Jean Sablons, the Salt of Alsace. Is that all I have left of my adventure? Sorry. No litigation. In this region of Gorde. This is one more memory that's trying to come back. Does the weight of the gold in the ancient Afro symbols grow heavier with time? They lit the way for works of art, for cubicles, for futuriles, for express-trains, for the Bow-wows. New patterns, no need for frames, two hundred years of art down the bog. It was the real secret of the sunken road that went up in flames in the inns of craftsmanship. Geometrical decors don't have the magnifying power of lambery tiles. The reluctant fire-back facilitates the disposition of the coping-stones of repression. Repression—could that be the only word?

This clarity isn't the same as the strange light in foreign parts. Their minds transformed by the knowledge revealed by Moses and the prophets, have they managed to submerge the planispheres and the toy lorries? I can't know, now. I don't know anything, now. But I might well have wondered whether that would help to interpret existence. And yet I so often, oh, so often respected the categories I'd inflicted on myself, I'd implanted in my brain, but that's of no great importance. Just because I get a few vague ideas from time to time, that doesn't mean that I've swallowed the prie-dieu along with the eucharist. Never, never, never—and I've only just thought of this—it's only now come into my moth-eaten head, my head eaten away by the moths of ignorance . . . Well, the moths of ignorance, the mythical moths of ignorance, they are concerned, they are disconcerting. No, though; no, though; nothing is read, nothing is reread, nothing is worth vile.

Once upon a time, hidden among the bushes, there was an old washboard by the riverside. The washerwomen used to beat their white linen on it.

Genealogy is where we find emanations, emanations. No, genealogy is where we no longer find, where we have never found, emanations.

Ladies and gentlemen who don't exist, and you, the audience, who are a black hole, my exposition contains several important arguments, from which it follows that the saved saviour will save. That's all a lot of hog-wash. If there were any hogs to wash, or cows to milk, we'd do it. Have there been manisteries, some manusferies, some matisferies, some mysteries and their acolytes who have messed the whole thing up?

Oh, my head, my head! As I go on talking, I notice that words say things. Do things say words? Why were we given heads? Questions aren't dead, then. I'm going to ask one: Rise, take up thy bed, and walk, Matthew, put on blue shoes, put the cages in sages, get on with your sewing, your heels with socks. The doctrine of the last days of the earth is going round in circles in the heavens, but the sewers are catching up with them. The sewers are blue and yellow flowers. They are used as oriflammes in public celebrations, in the field of universal speculation.

I don't know. All I know is that I have kept scraps and crumbs of cells on me.

I don't know.